ONLY THE HARDEST PUZZLES

D1385013

ONLY THE HARDEST PUZZLES

A VEXING VARIETY OF CROSSWORDS, SUDOKU & MORE

WILLA CHEN

ROCKRIDGE
PRESS

Dedicated to Sean, Bryant, Mommy, and Daddy.
Thank you for lifting me up, in every part of life and every day.

Interior and Cover Designer: Eric Pratt
Art Producer: Tom Hood
Editor: Clara Song Lee
Production Editor: Rachel Taenzler
Author photo by Ling Chen

Designed by Creative Giant Inc., Mike Thomas, Chris Dickey

ISBN: Print 978-1-64611-331-6

CONTENTS

INTRODUCTION   vii

PUZZLES

Crosswords   1

Word Searches   45

Sudokus   77

Calcudokus   101

Kakuros   125

Cryptograms   149

Cryptogram Clues   161

ANSWERS

Crosswords   162

Word Searches   168

Sudokus   173

Calcudokus   179

Kakuros   184

Cryptograms   190

FURTHER PUZZLING   194

INTRODUCTION

While Justin was walking down the street, a stranger shot him. Justin did not die, nor was he hurt or injured. Why not?

Third grade was the year I first discovered puzzles. Our bubbly teacher, full of idiosyncratic education ideas in her first year on the job, assigned us a steady stream of math, logic, and lateral thinking puzzles of the Justin-was-shot-by-a-stranger variety. I devoured them all. And I often found myself scouring the public library shelves for more.

I later latched onto puzzling as a sort of team adventuring hobby. In my college years at Princeton, I started an annual competition inspired by MIT's famous Mystery Hunt. Teams race to solve dozens of puzzles, which collectively lead to a secret answer location on campus. Nowadays I run a website called Mission Street Puzzles, an online analog with hundreds of teams globally competing in each 12-week season.

Why do we love puzzles? They stretch your mental muscles, keep your cognitive faculties sharp over time, and help you bond with loved ones over a shared challenge. For instance, the escape room—a group entertainment genre that usually involves solving puzzles to escape a locked room—has recently achieved mainstream popularity across generations, with clientele including families, millennials, and corporate groups. My own grandparents frequently text our family's group chat with deceivingly intractable math puzzles, often prefaced with "Here's a typical Chinese elementary school arithmetic problem." They may be onto something: A 2011 study suggested that solving crossword puzzles could delay dementia.

In this book, you'll find several types of classic puzzles, spiced up with some fresh ingredients.

The opening pages of each chapter will be a bit easier, to help familiarize you with each puzzle type—but remember, most of these are intentionally difficult! A good puzzle should put up a fight. It should stump you at times, yet its tricks should feel fair in the end. It should mesh together elegantly. And above all, the solver should eventually feel a sense of cathartic pride in unlocking the final solution. I love the process of writing a great puzzle that achieves these things, and truly hope you will experience the joy of puzzle-solving in these pages.

A final note on this book: It's yours to play with, write in, and enjoy. Feel free to skip around if you wish, or dive right into chapter 1. Happy solving!

P.S. And what about Justin? He is doing just fine: The stranger shot him on a camera.

CROSSWORDS

Crossword puzzles have been a staple of American newspapers since the first one appeared in the *New York World* in 1913. In a canonical crossword puzzle, you are presented with an empty grid like this: ⟶

Your mission is to fill in each white cell with a single letter. Each horizontal or vertical series of consecutive white cells—when read left-to-right or top-to-bottom, respectively—will spell a word, phrase, or abbreviation. Alongside the grid will be a list of clues for those words:

Across

1. Purple fruit

5. Something to dig

6. Cute water mammal

7. Another cute water mammal

Down

1. Haunter

2. ___ memorization

3. Spot for offerings

4. Outside of an orange

For this example, the solution would be: ⟶

We'll begin with some straightforward crossword puzzles like this one. Alternatively, if crosswords are old hat to you, then you may enjoy some of the variants later in the section. Let's get started!

CLASSIC

Let's start with a straightforward crossword puzzle example, with no strings attached. Using the numbered clues, can you fill out the crossword grid on page 3?

Across

1. Not classic
3. Locale
6. Flower's plumage
10. Little bit of earth
12. It's a red
14. It can be classical
16. It's sold by firmness
17. Note in 14
19. Big wader
20. Source of fiber
21. Crack
23. The classically?
24. Make contribution
26. President's family name, originally
28. Confuse
29. Violent group
31. Expel
34. Wes's collaborator
35. Classic romance
38. Manual organ
39. Skater-turned-designer
40. Forest constituent
41. Expectations, for short
44. Muffin deliverer's street name
45. Boot attachment
47. Bury
50. Sporting a pattern
52. With the most racket
55. Group of policy-makers
56. Astrid Leong-Teo portrayer
58. Zips home
59. Sparkling water's birthplace
60. Fish homes

DOWN

1. John of game theory
2. Weakling
3. In addition
4. Where you might go before camping
5. Time disambiguation
6. Text style
7. Fantasy character
8. Scoring event
9. Long hike, for short
11. Replace
13. Kidnapping victim Glazer
15. Sweet sauce
17. Disgraced
18. Add
22. Fictional courier
25. Current situation?
26. Last chance to eat
27. Ruthless leader
30. Fly
32. Current situation
33. Stops
36. Creeper
37. Beach book
42. 36-year constituent of 55
43. Chord
44. What's served
45. Fight
46. Fatty diet
48. Classic winter holiday
49. Squalor of *Unfortunate Events*
51. Expensive printer materials
53. AMZN cloud cluster
54. Dance with buffalo and Cincinnati steps
57. Negative

A completed crossword grid with the following filled-in letters:

Across
1. WEAR
5. ALARM
10. ARE
13. IAGO
14. LICHI
15. RANS
17. FROOT LOOPS
19. LIRA
20. END
21. AINT
22. REASON
24. CUES
25. PUNTING
26. BICEPS
29. HOLDEN
30. ABODE
31. JAMES
32. BEE
35. TIRE
36. RASED
37. PRAY
38. SSN
39. PELTS
40. SLATE
41. FLEECE
43. TONED
44. ATLATLS
46. SOD
47. CHAISE
48. WTO
49. O
51. EEKS
52. COCOAPUFFS
55. R
57. MEL
58. TAINT
59. FIAT
60. OSA
61. SKATE
62. OTRA

ISN'T IT ROMANTIC

Across

1. Famous mouse
5. 1's lover
10. Scottish lake
13. Biological waste product
15. Painful event caused by an insect
16. Happily
20. ___ true love
21. Marriages
22. More fit
24. ___ meets girl
25. Ukrainian city
26. Apple of my ___
27. Open to all genders
29. Full
30. Sci-fi romance movie
31. Sweetie ___
32. Checkered battleground
33. Emotionally close
35. Quick kiss
37. False statement
38. More adorable
39. Bunch of flowers
40. Bob of the head
41. Field full of proofs
44. Meeko of Pocahontas
47. Romantic novel
49. Jack Skellington's lover
50. Just fine
53. Absorbed
54. Free
57. Dips
58. Type of drink

DOWN

1. Angry crowd
2. Comes twice before "baby"
3. Betray, in relationship
4. Interdependency
6. Crush
7. Invalidate
8. Not on the Internet, for short
9. Cartoon donkey
11. Term of endearment
12. ___ ___ ___ ___ hold
14. Fancy food
17. Lovelorn but smelly character
18. Question asked to potential valentine
19. Salsa's partner
21. The Ring, to Gollum
23. Long fish
28. Chase
31. Workout bike
34. Obsessed
36. The heart is one example
38. Disturbing
42. 17 is one, as is 44
43. Reckless
45. Where you might get 15
46. Embraces
48. Extreme modesty
51. Pants
52. Evil one
55. Reduce
56. Intro to alternate name

FIVE RINGS

For this puzzle, you're given a batch of clues for the four words in each of the five overlapping "rings." Can you sort out the clue order and fill in all the rings?

Note #1: All words will be spelled left-to-right and top-to-bottom, as they are in a standard crossword.

Note #2: As you can see, the clues for each batch are alphabetized. Therefore, the clue ordering given is not significant in determining the answer ordering within the grid.

Top-Left Ring
- Desire
- Risk manager
- The university universe
- Timeless

Top-Right Ring
- Guy
- Hueless
- Make certain
- Untrue

Middle Ring
- Famous sculptor
- Required
- Separation or termination
- Telescope home

Bottom-Left Ring
- Cheerful
- Difficult situation
- Grown or found nearby
- Oversized

Bottom-Right Ring
- Make fun of
- Spinning amusement park fixture
- V-shaped icon
- XIX

SIX RINGS

Let's step it up a notch! This one is similar to the "Five Rings" puzzle, but with more rings.

Top-Left Ring
- Area for preliminary work
- Movement backward
- Ornament
- Type of amphibian

Outer-Middle Ring
- Non-tropical, non-polar area
- One interested in anicent society
- Preference developed gradually
- Region containing Ukraine

Bottom-Left Ring
- Ability to go from point A to B
- One might have these after viewing *The Ring*
- Studies
- Ursa Minor

Top-Right Ring
- Lush biome
- Only mildly relevant
- Playground sport
- Traffic circle

Inner-Middle Ring
- Have you considered . . .
- Reckless person
- Top of pants
- Type of foul

Bottom-Right Ring
- Container
- Credible testifier
- Fairy-tale family members
- Post-career life

SEVEN RINGS

Ready for one more ring? You can do it!

A
- Impossible fantasy
- Natural home
- Poor handwriting, casually
- Where cases are revisited

B
- (I'm) completely fed up
- Famous inventor
- "Quietly," for example
- US President

C
- The Bible, for example
- Too sweet
- Quick way to leave
- Santa Claus

D
- Copying from the web
- Highest two-dice outcome
- Ransacked
- Thrilling hobby

E
- Investigation
- Soothsayer
- Stare at accident
- Thrived

F
- Echo, for short
- Fruit breakfast pastries
- (It would be) irresponsible
- Violent American historical event

G
- Desserts served in glasses
- Familiarity ___ ___
- Smoothie maker
- Without a shirt

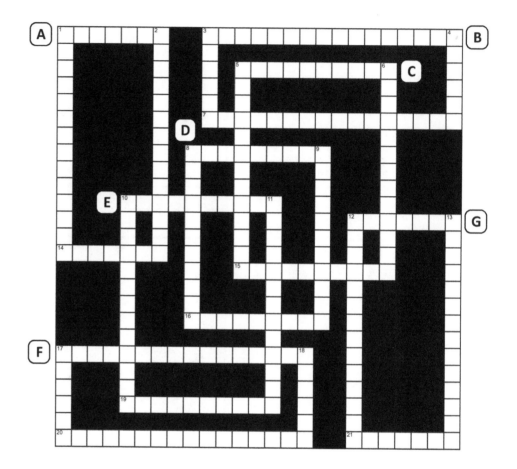

EIGHT RINGS

Even more rings—can you handle it?

A
- Bit of water
- Humble farmer
- Nuisance
- Stuffed pasta

B
- Ahi
- Charitable person
- Study of the signs
- Type of flower

C
- A type of nut
- Coating for the aforementioned nut, sometimes
- Crazed
- Slant

D
- Dada, for example
- Day that may exist, depending on month
- Spell
- Kill

E
- Education option for jobholders
- Good at making do
- Place to get hair done
- Torero

F
- Full of life
- Happenings to behold
- Middle Eastern place
- Self-triggering

G
- Like an octopus
- Mass of people
- Occurrence
- Wacky

H
- Ghost
- Overly catchy tune
- Place for relief
- Undermine

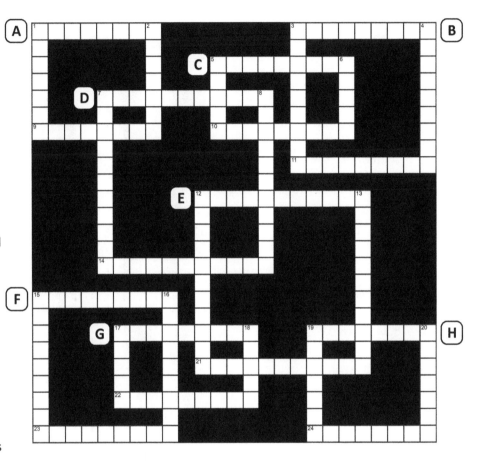

TEN RINGS

Ready for an even tougher challenge? This time, each ring's clues are mixed up with another one's. For example, the eight clues for the two "upper left" rings are mixed together into a single clue list. Can you sort them out?

Top-Left Rings

- Comes after three, two, one
- In anguish
- Non-experimental branch
- Redundant driver's location
- Speaking while unconscious
- Swap spots
- Type of outdoor maintenance service
- Walked with attitude

Top-Right Rings

- Accept with a positive frame of mind
- Baby
- Broke, slightly
- Coin
- One who covers last night's game
- Sweater
- Watery branches
- Wing-flapping machine

Middle Rings

- Chemistry container
- Controlled falling
- Drawings
- Famous crossing's site
- Lyrics before "you know it"
- Measurer of warmth
- Professional helping injuries heal
- The Dalai Lama, for instance

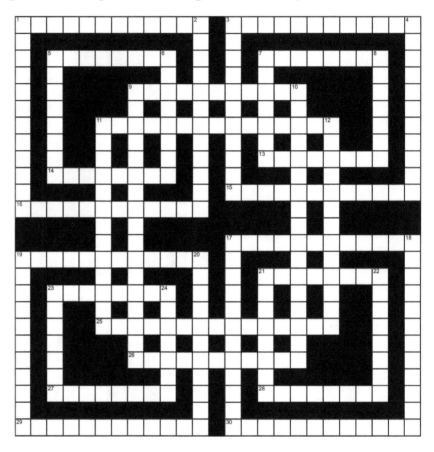

Bottom-Left Rings

- Do things innovatively
- Grow
- Endings
- Explode
- Renowned
- Road surface
- Secret communication line
- They're paid at a funeral

Bottom-Right Rings

- Bing, for instance
- Called, alternating registers
- Grandness
- Mistake-prone
- Planned payments
- Rap song and its artist, on the century's best-selling album
- Study of timber
- Western actor-turned-mayor

DON'T SHOOT THE MESH-ENGER

In this puzzle, each row and column contains multiple answers, in the order given. There are no spaces between consecutive answers. As an example, the clue "Animal that meows // Positive emotion // Animal that says woof" might correspond to the answer "CATHAPPINESSDOG."

Across

1. Light-colored vegetable // F-150, for example // Sweet snack
10. (Robin's) Tuck's occupation // Chameleon's skill // Look quickly
11. Short piece // Flatbeds, for example, in the UK // Winged animal // Climbing accessory
12. Extinct mammal // Victory // Measuring more in one dimension
13. Infant // Thing to watch // Similar
14. Fatty // Wish to have been otherwise // Foot holders
15. Statue material // Depart suddenly // Man without manhood
16. October holiday // Releasing heat
17. Allocate (e.g., money) // Very small // Small person // Famous storyteller

Down

1. Hot drink // Savory stuffed pastry // Dirty, conceptually
2. Type of reptile // Weird // Swinging object
3. Spotted // Falling-block game // It's like a spice, but leafy // Violent event
4. Contradiction // This kind of food is eaten when one's stressed out // Demand
5. Lottery // List of works quoted // Purchase
6. South American country // Dreamlike visions or spooky show
7. Queen's significant other // Award for questionable scientific achievements // Ledge
8. Animal used for charango // Oblivious // Staple food
9. Alpine activity // Talk about // Jerk of the diaphragm

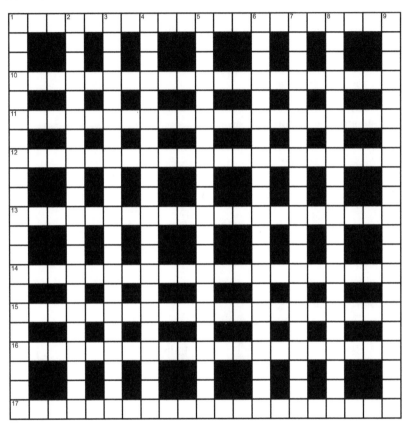

BIG MESH

The rules for this puzzle are the same as those for "Don't Shoot the Mesh-enger" (page 15). Good luck!

Across

1. Young person // Looney Tunes sign-off
13. Very rich person // Nickname for France-UK route // Intestinal bacteria
14. Pull // Place to sleep // Furry animal of the Late Pleistocene period
15. Vitamin A1 // Famous princess // Ninth of game // Yes, very casually
16. Annual event // Noodle soup // Young lady, or most expensive cow // Historical ship
17. Unique (phrase) // Move faster // Breakfast food
18. Gym activity // Rapper with a childish name // Flying vehicle
19. Mexican resort city // Interjection of mistake // Mercy // Shade
20. Initial-based poem // Mouth muscle // Hasty
21. Widespread language // Christian Bale's skill // Exit // Throat-clearing sound
22. Stevie Wonder song // Funny // Type of airplane
23. Graphite remover // Bangladesh currency // Influential mathematician-scientist // Plate-shaped instrument

Down

1. Referee // Area above pelvis // Truce
2. Required // Roosevelt who wrote "My Day" // Landlocked country
3. Award-winning rapper // Japanese theater style // Veer ___ ___ // Published instance
4. Beautiful place in New York City // Surprise
5. African capital // Spinach pie // Timekeeper
6. Kicking-based martial art // Christmas treat // Perfect
7. Drug inspiring desire // Sand vehicle // Small dog's sound
8. Solitary // Facial feature // Hanging out pointlessly // Unconscious state
9. Welsh symbol // Fictional scream-collecting business // Desire to consume
10. Pricing strategy charging for extra features // Lake in the Andes // Italian home of David
11. Part of kidney // Pop-prone object // Head scarf
12. Clean shot // City near Lake Michigan // Go back and forth // Low-key lodging

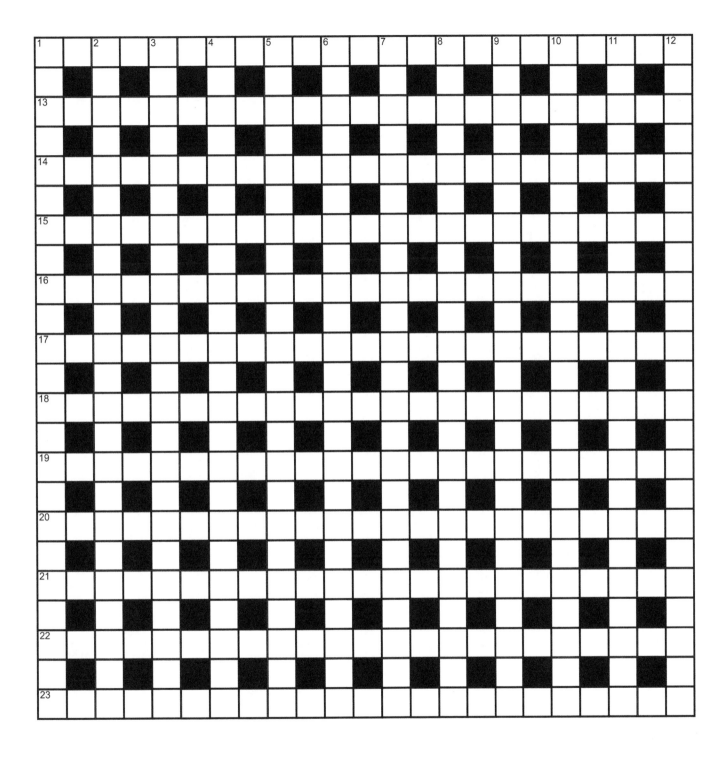

FUN AND GAMES

See "Don't Shoot the Mesh-enger" (page 15) for the rules for this type of crossword puzzle.

Across

1. 4x4 word game // Liquid holder // Space in 23 across game // Sharp // ___ Who?
13. Gruff // Scaffolding // Not pretty
14. Children's board game // Hand joints // Deprive
15. Without dissent // I ___ ___ Walrus // Type of housing
16. Make tidy // Make (the game) unfair // Grow // Pac-Man's home
17. Heater // Classic board game // Cow food
18. Die dot // Yelp like a pig // Matter // Arizona city
19. Chute's counterpart // Become healthier // Color between purple and red
20. Laugh // Indecision // Type of hat
21. In Clue, the number of cards in the envelope // Game of indirect communication // Classic strategic game // Military game
22. Toxic element // Negative reaction // Hair clip
23. Purdue student // Winner-takes-all game // Opposite of base

Down

1. Simple // Signature // Indoor lighting unit
2. One of the four colors in 10 down // Worn out // Member of black suit // Fancy car
3. Slender // Kingly animal // Costume party // Game involving retirement
4. Holiday spice // Move quickly // Etched // Mother
5. Festive procession // Word game // Illegal chatter
6. Not present // ___ the Gathering // Collude // Person ascending a mountain
7. Words of song // Tile shapes in 12 down game // Legendary beautiful woman // Ring
8. Simon & Garfunkel song // Half of a winter accessory // Famous puppet
9. Yesterday, according to Rebecca Black // Pair // Confuse // Frozen dessert
10. Visitor // A shelving unit, for example // Holy // Game with four pawn colors
11. Ballerina painter // First VP // Treatment style addressing the whole person
12. Speak // Resource-trading Eurogame // Massage

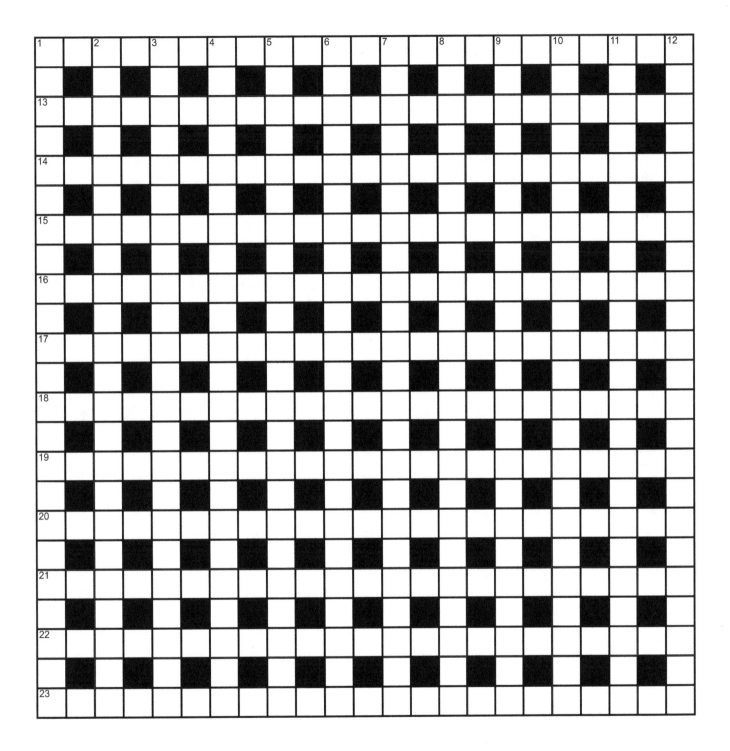

EAT YOUR VEGGIES

See "Don't Shoot the Mesh-enger" (page 15) for the rules for this type of crossword puzzle.

Across

1. Purplish vegetable // Tropical fruit // "Heady" vegetable // First man
13. Cooking directions // Animal, after being hit // Applying everywhere
14. Taste // Lima's country // Relating to smell // Manager
15. Stinging animal // Lock up // Bitter vegetable
16. Law // Study of mental disorders // Rubbish
17. Lustful // Smell // Light green vegetable // ___ and span
18. Hearted vegetable //Little kids' game // Empty
19. Ambiguous // Leafy vegetable // Mosque leader
20. Kitchen storage area // Root vegetable // Boat weight
21. Video game: *Gears* ___ ___ // Troubled // Someone else's words
22. Espresso drink // "Fruity" clothing store
23. Fast cat // Guitar-like instrument // Deep-fried Southern dish

Down

1. Taxes // Pen-shaped vegetable // Dull
2. Type of grain // "Vegetable" that's technically a large berry // Unit of butter // Not in any place
3. Unplanned // Magic practitioner // Creative person
4. Assistant // Leafy vegetable
5. Small vegetable // Person who might fix epilepsy // Written material found in classroom
6. Hairy animal // Type of fish // Water-packed vegetable // Horseshoe, for example
7. West Coast state // Cook in oven // Location of famous riots
8. Italian appetizer // Japanese pumpkin
9. Southwestern state // Legend // "Vegetable" that's technically a fruit // Men's underwear
10. Each // Crunchy vegetable // Cowboy's accessory // Leap
11. Act of ditching // Ready to harvest // Comfortable seat // Top of thigh
12. Dark syrup // Yes, in Spain // Two-hulled boat // Hurting

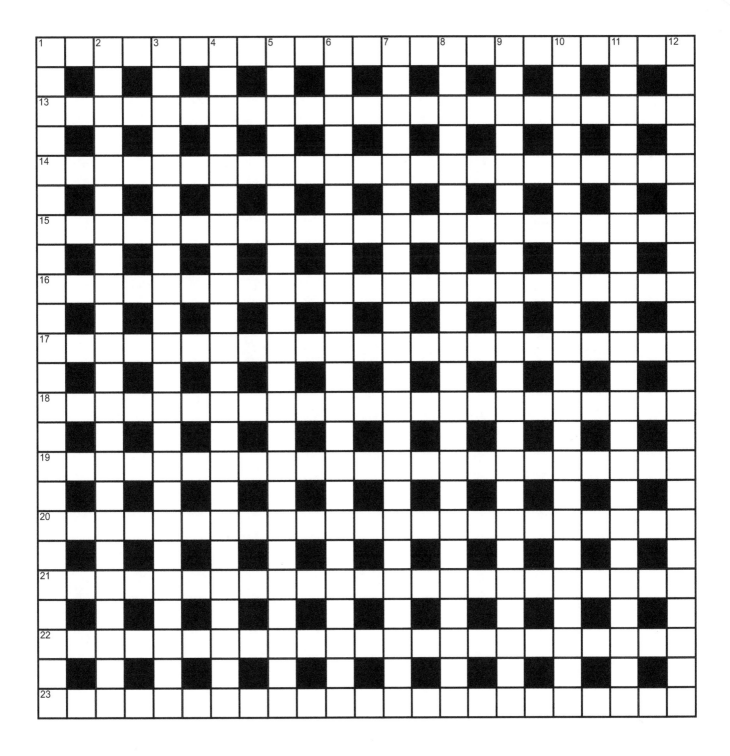

SPACE MESH

See "Don't Shoot the Mesh-enger" (page 15) for the rules for this type of crossword puzzle.

Across

13. Planet // Contagious illness // Futuristic genre

14. Dark patch on a bright background // Trustworthiness // Exact

15. 3-D images // Archer in the stars // Dwarf planet

16. Large star // Solar element // Fake grass

17. Debbie Downers // Planet // Eight-legged creepy-crawly

18. Nighttime illumination // Orbital measurement // Display bottom to

19. Rocket Man Elton // It makes it hard to breathe // What's above the troposphere

20. Car or cat // Video website // Small bird // Type of satellite

21. Medical wing of starship // Sudden crisis // Slippery sport

22. Card's "Game" player // Shooting star // Planet // Tough ordeal

23. Place to get a car // Undress // Worldwide enforcement organization

24. Moon of Jupiter // Very fast // Planet // Shakiness

Down

1. Planet // Rich // Our planet makes one per day // Serious criminal

2. Ear instrument // Space visitor // Leg joint // Hang around silently

3. Support // Not radical // Countless

4. A little at a time // A district of London or NYC // Vacuum cleaner // Sesame product

5. Infraction // 4-D figure // Field of flight

6. Merging // Astronomical instrument // Dipper size // Planet

7. Fear // Type of bulb // Natural show in the sky

8. Supernatural // Planet // What exists // Shooter // Atomic scientist

9. Lineups // Third-party initiator of romance // Anti-pain medicine

10. Of this world // Piece of work // Hinged slab // Come back

11. Guess // Legend of Hollywood // Home ENTMT

12. God of the sky // Planet // Chemical in hand sanitizer

A LITTLE CRYPTIC

In the American-style crosswords you've seen in this book so far, each clue simply provides a definition (or, generally, semantic description) of the corresponding answer term. By contrast, in a cryptic crossword, popular in the UK, each clue is a two-parter: it combines (1) a definition with (2) a wordplay characterization of the answer. This is best demonstrated with an example:

A typical cryptic clue for the word POLITE might be "Well-mannered American poet, housing on fire."

In this case, "Well-mannered" is the definition. As a rule, the definition always comes at the very beginning or the very end of the cryptic clue.

The rest of the clue will be the wordplay. In this example, POE (American poet) is "housing" (containing) the word LIT (synonym for "on fire").

A few more tips and convention:
- Punctuation in the clue text can generally be ignored.
- Words like "muddled" and "destroyed" often signal anagrammed letters.
- An exclamation mark at the end of the clue means that the full clue is both the definition and the wordplay characterization.

It seems tricky if you're unfamiliar with the genre, but you'll get the hang of it! On the next page is a small example to get you started.

Across

1. Dad leases dads
7. Solitary shelled animal without ab
8. Fix again: level of detail, for short, and sound of disgust
9. Speaker is damp without sun vitamin
10. Between truth and dare, an unending orb
12. Bird, after a forked bone: wailing cry
14. Quick touch is a quick touch back
16. Damaged oar: it's a profit calculation
17. A smatter with the middle replaced is more clever

Down

1. Standard decays birds
2. Drink kale without potassium
3. Famous parks really only stay available as an acronym
4. Uninitiated gene before my rival
5. A Welsh city is a confused pro surrounded by . . . lizard
6. Student: bottomless hole in scar
11. Pickup truck tramp with no ends
13. Despair swooned without odd letters
15. Dad is short pal

A BIGGER CRYPTIC

Now that you've gotten acquainted with the cryptic crossword genre, how about a heftier challenge?

Across

1. Big animal confused "Heel!" and "Pant!"
4. Weight sounds like a murder measurement device
9. Work backward: iron stronghold
10. Undo crazy shirt loop (as in a car)
11. Idiot Remus's head in a moon
14. Covering with amp, instead of oversleeping outdoors
15. Instrument is on (between two grams)
16. Obvious program: a lease
17. Dirty players start old, holding stringed instrument
19. "Celestial formation" contraption, with trap replaced by a beer
25. One more ant hero dissembled . . .
26. Scattered skis make a show of affection
27. Go inside a damaged argyle statue
28. Big loss in natural fuel

Down

1. Native dispersed mice den
2. Witty saying about pig is mare running backward
3. Neighbors' start after own safe place
5. Animal, before Internal Domestication Enterprise starts compound
6. Cunning—with initial changed—is said of water, appliances, and athletes
7. Nitrogen in an atom, all up state
8. Delicate and fragile, without middle or end
12. Strong in confused teens
13. Always goes in last, I tell you, all initially for speed
18. Massive bulking uses hydrogen in place of boron
19. Damaged crate or god
20. Radiant, beheaded flight
21. Ones with no beginning or end: me and sis rival
22. Silly Six (or Four!) in trial
23. "Music-maker" is an inside job, destroyed
24. Horned animal I found in shattered horn

CRYPTIC CRYPT

Now you're getting the hang of these cryptic crosswords!

Across

1. A no thanks after a company scarf
4. Accomplish: vie badly, in pain
7. Clean twisted curbs
10. Before mailed, in attendance
11. Perplex, not add
13. Pen kept center muscle
15. Sounds of a German car: none
16. Throb on the edges around a sound digit
18. Marked as stupid without two vowels
21. Sounds like a boy in a Disney movie
23. Stay in touch—a wanderer following a monster and a spot with any center
24. A mole: unrestricted about tickles without commitments
26. Comets connected with ugly sore
29. From Peru in packaging
30. Real confused around zero, so spray
31. After a messy tour, able without a worry

Down

1. Sound of a spelling event and pin head
2. Hurt cooler guy
3. A stray with hunger's start inside smoker's bin
4. Desert a boycott to dress
5. Starts however often Rent names an instrument
6. Listeners: muddled eras
8. Seat Franklin on the fronts of carriages and horses
9. Record Dumbledore cut short by a million
12. Approaches a car in cased in a bad condition
13. Thud and jeer tall plant
14. Item for sale favors a type of tape
16. Crime won't end logic
17. Pacific island is created, with Europe's and Oceania's beginnings
19. Gut: meat head in an abode demolished before start of night
20. Reckless person is an attorney and crimson, evil
21. Flat men, before time and after a piece
22. Create Democrat first lady before cut
24. "Friend," to start, ate up cheese
25. Half-ass's codes
27. Mexican sandwich is a wrinkled coat
28. Yes: "daze end" amount

PUT A SPIN ON IT (CRYPTIC)

Here's another cryptic. Give it a whirl!

Across

1. Treks afar, with sis around
5. Hanging thing's end in pant
10. Drummer circle, and another circle
11. Judge Grater lacks gravity
12. Final two-thirds of arcane stick
13. Are in front of a region
14. She meets the heads of Enron and Pfizer to get farm animals
16. Plush toy company hosting wedding that has no wing for a plush toy
20. The solver framed by #4 is a failure
21. Awful murder containing a rather "instrumental" body part
24. The rudest royal hides ruin
26. What a volcano did is treed-up, damaged
29. Gay around a wet, rowdy entrance
33. A Greek character makes stirred tea
35. In Disneyland, beauty sounds like a ringer
37. Paces confusingly to get to promontories
40. Tube with neon removed: a reversed epipen
41. Not applicable: Zimbabwe as member of a particularly reprehensible socialist group
42. "CLASSICALLY, 'HEY!' IN HAWAIIAN" is a permutation of "WAY I, A CHILEAN, SAY, 'HI!' IN CALLS"
43. An Asian country in 24 horas
44. In sunbed, is tan - terribly far off
45. Evergreen leaves need less, with no sulfur

Down

2. Lets go! A pine tree on the Spanish domain
3. Full-spectrum anger has its end at the beginning
4. Rewritten code ops, to have picked up the story before a rival
5. Stolen between 3-rated and 4-rated
6. Well-known, not embarrassing condition
7. A display of augmented reality and a light beam
8. Vine wrapped around a carbon copy for preventative medicine
9. A rascal--Remy--has no head for school
15. Locks openings of huge and imposing rotors
17. Fathers are barely-passing advertisements, for short
18. A backwards, spoken-word song comprises the expected performance
19. She is excluded from washer combat
22. Dunk without a corrupted iPad
23. Moaned in need of one maniac
24. Pet's confused master
25. Thing holding ball there, having only odds
26. Cover up a jumped lisp: interjecting between half an echo, and half of that
27. Employ an electrical device, cut short from the front
28. Sharp member of four is shod, with all four shifted forward by one
30. A long read about medicine's beginning: a toe
31. First half of winter spells come first
32. Shouting yearling undergoes same transformation as Barack becoming black
33. Fancy element moving letters from Maine to Georgia
34. Sell gold cat without a lion, missing 50
35. Be an illness ender, for edible seeds
36. Note: Under loo is a scrubber
38. Paraguay parent is regarding after a pad
39. Slain, dismembered mollusk

CRYPTIC TRIPTYCH

Across

1. Copay without a domestic animal follower
5. Rear rib, broken, is an obstacle
9. Evergreen con, if in front of emergency room
12. Peace with two norths, surrounding a remorseful feeling
13. Place to wash butt and ab, all mixed up, with an hour inside
14. Stout in front of a domed room
15. Beam in the middle of frays
16. Poor, bald, lacking: 50
17. A tinier, disorganized, sedentary tendency
18. In parasol, art of the sun
19. Hell is in oxygen after a fern
20. Every evening, rightly has replaced robe's front with negligee's
21. Punches shamrocks, without harm
22. California cost is just a whim
25. Try, after a computer science notation, to get bias
28. Carriage input/output in a chart
30. Elegant flowers sag in the center
32. Woman with no character to start a Middle-Eastern country
33. One Roosevelt, one real muddle
34. Toward the interior of Pinto without pressure
37. Shrunk in, I'm reversed
38. Embedded in gold, i.e. classic song
40. Indian dress is owned by Ira when reversed
42. Leveling is a dark time
43. Desert creature came before lizard's head
44. Shape of California locale: label in operation
46. Disturbed Sue; AC/DC blamed
49. Keepsake within an brief notice: a net is tangled
51. Inside a mare, what in Spain is a prominent sign
54. A stirred sap becomes a relaxing place
55. P.M. is an example; A.M. is around an accomplice
57. Attain ghetto's odds
58. Drool a liter in a crying person
59. A big stick is half the battle
60. Be laced, tangled disaster
61. Before listeners, Instagram or Tinder shows up
62. One army messed up at the present time
63. Tiny machine reengineered on baton
64. Speak directly to promotion clothing
65. A period of time is a gem, without a minute
66. Set of supplies found inside-- prepack it.

Down

1. A brief explanation describes destroyed Pontiac
2. In openness is found pasta
3. Activity for founding fathers
4. Extended treatment starts the rap years
5. Watch a child in bait, by son's head
6. Eternal task is reshuffled to get a viper
7. Social exchange is half of barter, in the middle of inaction
8. Bone going down meets snob going up for hair accessories
9. Famous rapper "B" and B's neighbors of the heart
10. Better finger, without a gram
11. An "inside castle piece," then natural base colony, on an island
23. I hide in a party for equality
24. Vain, broken, terrible leader
25. Brie containing own dessert
26. A log, destroyed, is the target
27. Yes, an overhang is gaping
28. See clan confused; purge
29. North Carolinian mixed up her tale
30. Stylish, long before Midwestern city
31. Late, confused, and charged thing: happiness
35. Metropolises are shortages without a scar
36. Basking in the absence of ski noise
38. Philosopher of shaving

fame in the midst of
ad-hoc camping

39. Evil spirit's smashed-
treat exhibit

41. Speaker precedes kind
caricature

45. A singleton gone,
without gravity

46. A group on recklessness

47. In fun, one!

48. The most stupid is the best,
after mud goes up

49. State, not a man, shuffled

50. Cosmos, without a century,
is a gradual absorption

51. Mom's roadster,
a beautifying tool

52. Clear the way: a headless
outdoor protective lotion

53. Very serious sound
receiver: Nest

56. Take illegally, in bird

57. Big clothing store or big hole?
Sullivan of TV stared

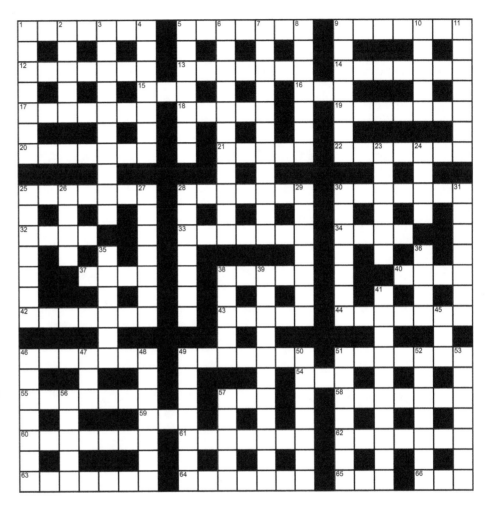

ALPHABET GAME

Across

3. Five-letter bird, the last three of which are ill
5. Six-letter attractor, the last three of which ensnare things
9. Nine-letter clothing item, the last three of which are a body part
12. Nine-letter opener, the last four of which are a group of people
13. Eight-letter beautifier, the last four of which are a small blood-feeder
15. Seven-letter officer, the first four of which transmit naturally
17. Six-letter body part, the first three of which are a child
19. Six-letter color, the first four of which are a shout
21. Five-letter body part, the last three of which are a musical helper
23. Nine-letter music-maker, the last three of which are a number
25. Six-letter country, the last three of which are a route
26. Five-letter mammal, the last three of which are supportive clothing

Down

1. Five-letter flower, the last three of which are a body part
2. Six-letter mammal, the last three of which are a small amount
4. Six-letter clothing item, the first four of which are a heavy lifter
6. Eight-letter food, the first four of which are grainy
7. Nine-letter recreational object, the first four of which are thrown at it
8. Seven-letter bird, the first three of which write
10. Seven-letter transmitter, the first four of which are a bet
11. Seven-letter body part, the first five of which are a kitchen tool
14. Seven-letter festive object, the last four of which are a bird
16. Seven-letter ingredient, the first four of which are a plant
18. Five-letter building, the last three of which are a room for private functions
20. Six-letter organism, the first three of which are a delight
22. Six-letter fruit, the last five of which are a span of values
24. Five-letter bird, the first four of which are a great person

SILLY SPIRAL

With the clues given (not necessarily in order), your mission is to fill in the white and gray spirals.
The cells marked with □ and • symbols also spell out special "spoke" words across the white and gray cells.
Note #1: All words will be spelled left-to-right and top-to-bottom, as they are in a standard crossword.

White Spiral
- Behave
- Enthusiastic participant
- Fast tempo
- Hexagonal structure
- Mahatma Gandhi's birthday
- Organism's food processing mechanism
- Out of the running
- Puzzle or riddle
- River home
- Spicy
- Start of story
- Throw
- Type of dot or dance
- Type of storm
- Whale expert

Gray Spiral
- Cancer cause and cure
- Common layout for typing
- Corpse
- Expert, for short
- Fun distraction
- Large person
- Pointy symbol
- Thing to hang your hat on
- Thunder clouds
- Timeless example
- Tireless
- Unwilling to communicate
- When the plane leaves

Vertical Spokes □
- Categories
- Decide where to reassign
- I came
- Path

Horizontal Spokes •
- Coy preview
- Roll
- Shield
- Type of flush

CROSS-REFERENCE CROSSWORD

Across

1. [10 across] that one would [26 across] with a [17 down]
4. Dive ungracefully
8. Name of state
10. Creature
11. Command to [9 down]
12. Mathematical symbol
14. Healthy
15. [34 down] of China
17. Display
19. Slope
21. Equip
22. Romantic [27 down]
23. [27 down] caretaker in famous [16 down]
25. Fun
26. Straightforward
28. Arrive
30. Slow [10 across]
32. Name of river
33. [47 across] [16 down] object
35. Dried grape
36. Alternative to LLC
39. [17 across]: ___ [41 across]
40. Large type of [27 down]
41. Contributor
43. Battling
45. [10 across]s kept at home
47. Common alloy
48. Cool
50. Motivated
51. [27 down] that can be smoked
53. Character in Belgian [15 down]
54. Average
57. Comes after [30 down]
59. Act of [29 down] [10 across]s into [45 across]
61. [65 across] per [67 across]
64. Energetic
65. Christian ritual
66. Program for a [52 down] to play a particular [25 across]
67. Level of [14 across]
68. Wicked

Down

1. Abundant
2. Symbol
3. Pieces
5. Type of paper
6. Disaster
7. Execute
8. Religious sister
9. Common [45 across]
12. It's sometimes found on the back of a [44 down]
13. Late
15. [64 across] [17 across]
16. Full of pleasant [14 across]
17. Spike worn on [11 across]
18. Dances
20. 150 [12 across] is 1 ___ ___ ___
23. [39 across] of [7 down]ing
24. City in [8 across]
25. Gull
27. Factory
29. Forming
30. Short unit of [63 down]
31. [21 across] muscles
34. Institution for policies
37. Hands on [48 across]s
38. Ability to direct a [65 across] of people
39. [27 down] seller
42. Change
44. [2 down] that's worn
46. [17 down] to action
49. [25 across] causing bruises
52. Young person
54. Stick to
55. Frozen
56. Gloomy
58. Cured [60 down]
60. [10 across] as food
62. Therefore
63. Pace

ANOTHER CROSS-REFERENCE CROSSWORD

Across

1. Movement of the [2 down]
5. Something hard to [38 across]
7. [72 across]
10. Joint
11. Go in
12. [7 across] College location
13. Seat for a [1 down]
15. Tumble
18. One of the [27 across]s
20. Not [48 down]
23. CV
25. To [63 across] ___
26. Red or green [46 down]
27. [20 across] object
28. Pre-[65 down] tool
29. [68 across] over
31. Do well in [80 down]
32. Type of [65 down]
34. First [33 down]
36. Emotional
38. [10 across] (burden)
40. [51 down] (British)
42. Brown [76 across]
43. Become knowledgeable
45. Secret [52 down]
47. Individual
50. Have meaning
53. Hurt
56. Messy [47 across]
58. Hit
59. Save up
61. What [46 down] may do over time
63. Conjunction
64. Play a [8 down]
66. ___scraper
68. Round of a [80 down]
70. [39 down] a [48 down] stretch
72. Threesome
73. Container for [77 down]
74. [66 across][15 across], for instance
76. Creature of the [66 across]
78. Egyptian city
79. [65 down] language
81. Excitement
83. Something one would [31 across]
84. From [12 across], for instance
85. This [47 across] received [21 down] for effects
86. Not latter
87. A [20 across] time
88. [39 down][37 down] of situation

Down

1. Band featuring Mr. [34 across]
2. Dirt
3. [86 across] nation
4. Impolite
5. Unwritten
6. Doing [53 across] to others
8. Part in [74 across]
9. Continuously
14. Lubricate
16. Yogurt [77 down]
17. Type of [76 across]s
19. Alligator, for example
21. [83 across] for [74 across]
22. State of [50 across]
24. [26 across] eater
25. Mistake
29. Prepare [46 down] with [14 down]
30. [61 across] a [47 across]
33. [2 down], e.g.
34. Mother
35. ___ end ([44 down])
37. Clue direction
39. Move quickly
41. Uninspiring
44. [51 down]
46. Fuel for [47 across]
47. Fictional [38 across]
48. Not tall
49. [39 down][37 down] housing
51. Donkey
52. Connection
54. [71 down]
55. A [57 down] has zero, a [47 across] has two
56. Move toward [66 across]
57. Type of [20 across] [19 down]
60. [47 across] that [29 across]s
62. Beginning
65. [26 across] product
67. Word said in the presence of good [46 down]
69. [58 across]s, [55 down], etc.
71. Strange
75. Too
77. [46 down] [63 across] ___
79. Tossing [80 down]
80. ___ of [13 across]s
82. Ice in [66 across]

IT'S THE FINAL CROSSWORD

Across

2. [37 down] natural
5. Royal sons
9. Approach
10. [42 down] for a [14 down]
11. In this [42 down]
13. A [15 across]
15. [90 across] or ___
17. Cast [44 across] on
19. Light [91 across]-[89 across]
20. [56 across] last [42 down]
21. [96 across] to [22 across]
22. [61 down] left by [8 down] object
24. [37 down] look [62 across] to
25. Something you [28 across]
28. [57 down] [91 across]
30. Teach to use [25 across]
32. Not [55 down]
33. Mail
34. Sad
36. [41 down] [36 down] [68 down]
43. Greatest degree, for short
44. [56 across] right [29 down]s
45. Spring [11 down]
47. US
48. [20 across] hair
51. [37 down] good
52. Simple
53. Arrange
56. Obtain
58. It has a [71 down]
59. It's taken in, in a [97 across]
60. That guy
62. [33 across] along
65. Identify
66. Denotes original [65 across]
67. Sacrificial son

69. Un-purchases
72. [69 across] to the [56 down]
73. [46 down] [58 across]
74. [68 down] metric
76. [37 down] [4 down]r
78. Pain medication
82. It's found in a [25 across]
84. Dodge
86. ___ room ([25 across])
88. From Havana
89. Fruit
90. Strike
91. Scarlet
92. [9 across] toward
93. Paddle
94. Small [53 down]
95. Buddy
96. Covet
97. Sign of being [55 down]

Down

1. Made fancier
2. [51 across]
3. Questionnaire
4. [37 down] yet [11 across]
6. Lizard
7. Important
8. Astute
9. [11 down] songs
11. [72 down] Day, for instance
12. A perfect cube
14. [34 across] Moon, for example
16. Digital assistant [65 across]
18. [15 across]ing the past
23. Draft again
26. Vegetable
27. [13 across]
29. Something you [33 across]
31. Belonging to them

35. [96 across]
36. [62 across]-looking action
37. It's ___ [52 across] being green
38. NE city
39. ___ or [37 down], [11 across] I [9 across]
40. Software [68 down]
41. Medical checks
42. Location
46. [37 down] hard
48. It [9 across]s before [12 down]
49. Manor [72 across]
50. Be aware of
53. Make up [65 across]
54. Filled
55. [82 across]ed
56. Made into [86 across]
57. Rotate
58. [75 down] event
61. Investor [88 across]
63. Raggedy ___
64. Inventor of [53 across]s
68. Presence of [95 across](s)
69. Harmony
70. It's worn by [15 across] [47 across]
71. Only
72. Work
75. [37 down] prose
77. Take [42 down]
79. Fashion
80. [65 across] of lake
81. Actor Murphy
83. [37 down] multiple
85. Moon of Jupiter
87. Marry

WORD SEARCHES

In a word search puzzle, a grid of random-looking letters will be presented to you; your task will be to find hidden words among those letters. The puzzle's difficulty can vary from very easy to quite difficult, depending on the specific size of the puzzle, orientation of the hidden words, and presence of a clue list. Because they are so accessible for all ages, word search puzzles are often used in classrooms as a fun mechanism for studying lists of vocabulary words, historical names, scientific terms, and so on.

ICE-CREAM SOCIAL

In the simplest type of word search, all words appear in straight lines (across, vertically, or diagonal). Sometimes, the words will be spelled in reverse—that is, from right to left, or from bottom to top. Can you find the ice-cream flavors hidden in this grid?

Banana
Birthday Cake
Black Sesame
Blue Moon
Butter Pecan
Coffee
Cookie Dough
French Vanilla
Hazelnut
Lemon Sorbet
Mint Chocolate Chip
Moose Tracks
Neapolitan
Orange Sherbet
Peanut Butter
Pistachio
Pumpkin Pie
Rocky Road
Rum Raisin
Salted Caramel
Spumoni
Stracciatella
Strawberry
Superman
Tiger Tail

```
O M P Y I C A K L I A T R E G I T A I E S R B M O
N T A E E A U B A N A N A I O R U M R A I S I N U
R A E S A F L A L L E T A I C C A R T S M I A S A
S R C A U N I H U R S M O R Y S A K U E N A I H C
O N F E E P U K O N M O N U R E R I N K O E N C I
O O B E P A E T C I A O H A T L R P S A O E O K K
T N B E B R M R B R C T K L A C E A N C M T M S A
E A S C O A E S M U T T Y N P S O D C Y E P U O O
A T A P A V T T U A T E U K I T C O U A U A P R E
C I A O T O I B T B N T C C H Y F N A D L E S A N
H L Y I T L C M P U T L E S C F S B M H B E R N H
F O R H L R T M A K B E C R E L A R N T O U O G G
R P R C T B I T T L E E D E T E L R C R T E L E U
E A E A F L M F T E M H E M A S T O O I R A A S O
N E B T L I I E E A U L E M L N E C M B P E T H D
C N W S R E C B S O I I O G O F D K R T T I L E E
H L A I T U M E O N A O A I C E C Y M C S P C R I
V R R P S K S O E U S R I S O T A R D C U N I B K
A T T S R K A A N E E C R K H N R O W T E I E E O
N C S E C S C R T S L E A O C F A A O G L K I T O
I A E A E O E R M A O P S I T T M D P C C P B S C
L M L W I M A P A C A R T U N L E Z A H K M L E T
L B E M R C L P S B M O B N I C L E A P A U T C B
A E U I K R C R E R I O E E M I K L C A H P L T E
R O I S Y L A D T F O A G O T K R E T C E H I L G
```

ANAGRAMS

This is a twist on a word search that uses anagrams. Each word in the list below has an anagram that is a regular English word, which appears in the word search. The clue itself does not appear in the grid; only the anagram. For example, "Airflow Clue" is a scrambled version of the word "Cauliflower," so you will need to find CAULIFLOWER in the word search grid.

Airflow Clue
Armada Boss
Die Starving
Dirty Room
Entire Term
Finer Roast
Flew Round
Hotel Price
Hotel Suite
Hymn Locale
Initial Cop
Late Bishop
Mercuric Fence
Moon Starer
Obtain Crust
Peel Radish
Rainy Tire
Rarest Tuna
Real Fun
Rogue Sand
Ruby Rebel
Runty Ivies
Scratch Ear
Soviet Line
Warm Voice

```
Y D I N L E E L E A D E R S H I P A D A O G S I C
M O I R D L Y R N N O N A I C I T I L O P C U M R
U U Y I N A R N A V F C R Y U L A L I T A V O N E
W O N D E R F U L R E R I U O S S N F N A R R O T
T S Y A S E A O C C E T S R T M A A W P N A E I P
Y U S D O N T I T S E A D R C L E O I E T E G S O
R B T V U U F E T T I O O R L U N R R E E N N I C
A T E E R F R T O I R N W A M T M O O L T H A V I
R R E R R M S E N M O T Y I E I N F W I R T D E L
E A M T I E R A I M M T R N T S M E E I E L L L E
N C I I H I R T E I E O E F S E A R M R I N T E H
I T C S Y E O R S O L N S O E B F P C E E P R T S
T I R I A R S T Y Y A F T R R C T I H I R N T T M
I O O N Y F A W O U N I A E E D A R O L C I C C B
S N W G T O R O S E C E U S A Y L N E P H I T E D
D D A O O F L V E G H L R T I O A A E I E I S E Y
T D V T N I E O T R O R A A Y R I N I T N R L A R
E P E O R R A M N S L L N H I V F S R O R S Y F R
L U R T U M R R I S Y F T C T U U M O O U O T L E
R B R R A T B T I I N R O D A S S A B M A R A R B
W I E I A E I R V A S T N A W E T Y N A I R B Y E
I E E O O R E W O L F I L U A C L R N R I I N E U
T H O S P I T A B L E E R S I L H O U E T T E I L
U U N N I Y N Y T I S R E V I N U O E B A E H L B
T S R D L H S E E U C I T S S R E T C A R A H C A
```

CHANGE FIRST LETTER

For each of these clues, one word is being transformed into another by changing just the first letter. For example, if the clue were "Type of precipitation ⟶ Understand" then the words SNOW and KNOW would appear in the word search.

Affectionate → Post on social media

Animal with antlers → Ill-fitted

Appendage → Stick around

Art → Pick

Bears or worms, for instance → Belly

Bicycle part → Physical award

Break → Even though

Devout woman → Title for man

Dialogue → Pre-cake

Dishonest person → Entertainment place

Easy → Bodily blemish

Flower part → Type of material

Get denser → Type of bird

Kind of dessert → Amateur

Mother → Album by the Who

Move water → Walk awkwardly

Opening → Direction

Place to put wallet → Type of accessory

Russian complex → Mischievous being

Roused → Small object

Sell → Interfere

Set aside → Have the right

Slender → Set of drinks

Tall feature → Water structure

Thin → Happiness

Thinking thing → Gutter

Cheerful → Transporter

Tree animal → Pack animal

Type of ceremony → Stuff slept on

Wrinkle → Lubricate

```
I A A T I F E L D D E P E S A E R C E I I L D G D
D D G D E P W E D D I N G O O I E D R A I N R L H
F K R I N E E L D D E M T B L R E T T A B S E A E
O E E D E T W R O L T P K U O U M S L M W S P T O
U R A I I I R T R L T O M M Y E E A R E Y G P E I
N P S E S M E N W P R E T A E H C E E C E E I M H
T P E I R E R E I E L P M I S N G T A C K S H E Y
A N T T R E I E P L N O F O I N O C K L N O S R H
I I C H E T G I S I M T E T I P S E R I O O Y I T
N A Y G T E E N A E E E T F E H I E E D M M M E U
E T E I A I M R I A R L R E T S I M W E E N M L O
T N K L E E B R S L S V D K D E S P I T E E O P S
H U N F H E O I E P R L E D G N I D D E B K M M E
G O O I T O S M N V O H E T A E E I M N A C M I L
I M D E K T P A B O R L C S N P T K M C I I P P D
L R K I E N O L S O E H F H I D F I R U N H M G D
S R E R A T A E G I I P Y E P L A G A I D T R C A
I M I L Y D N I K P E M M E C A R V S D C E R L W
W Y I M E S P O P N I C M R M D D A E H M D A O N
B S M P M O O E N E S I U R T E K P I L N L M C T
E U A E C C R T M K T V G E E M E C I T E C F K S
T K L K I R R K A O E L T H T T K N M F K H E E K
M N E E L C R E K W U O N A A E T L R A O E A T D
A T E T L T I R N T B T D L N Y T A R R T E E M E
P T T D E V R E S E D M H T A U R I P C H R L M P
```

CHANGE LAST LETTER

This time, one word is being transformed into another by changing its *last* letter. For example, if the clue were "Blue bird ⟶ Glass container" then the words JAY and JAR would appear in the word search.

Area near fire → Ample

Assault → Append

Be obsequious → Sesame Street character

Cash → Famous painter

Chart → Type of fruit

Cleaning implement → Flowing water

Coil → Bolt

Consecutive series → Flowing water

Enumerated → Pay attention

Flower substance → Survey taker

Go back over → Pull back

Implant → Glowing residue

Keep watch over an area → Supporter

Large bird → Stash

Layer → Domesticated animal

Lifted → Place above

Make low noise → Expanded

Make royal → Large group

Measurement device → Burn

Mick ___ → Not smooth

Nobleman → Create jet

Padding → Kind of restaurant

Pieces → Celebration

Put together → Organic material

Restricted eater → Hedonistic destination, for short

Take unfair shortcut → Inexpensive

Temporarily unseeing → Permanently unseeing

Type of crop → Something sought

Want for more → Color of nature

Wide hole → Boxes

```
G O L I S T E N M E R T N R W T G H F A E K C C E
L S E T O E R E R A L O E H N R R A U N T A M R E
I C S E T A R C R A R O R T S T O R E H R E E A O
A A T N A G E V R T E H O R O I W G Q C K R A T O
R L E Y B H O R A E S E F A H P L G A A M T N E G
G D R T G L E P R E B P R E P T S S O T R S E R B
T H E R B R R C L P R M R H T R L H C T E D E H L
C Q G A R T T P Q A G S E I Y E N O M A V E S P I
U E G E O S E E L R I D C V N R E D C C O E C A N
S G A H O O T T E G A G R T O G P J S A R R H R D
N Q J P M P L E V H A S O S W O E A A E G G E G D
V J U A A M R F O V S R W T L S H G G O O E A N E
S N D I G O B F R E R T N L C E R G E T O B P E B
A T N O R C O U G T G P E R A A O E V C V R L E M
L C W T H E S B J O M N O V R T I D W Y C O O R E
S A O E S O P M O C R W E E E T J T T R H O R G A
C R R K D E T S I L D N R T F A A E J M E K T S G
A T G N E N E A B A A S I G F C E N R N A E A L S
L E N I S S I E E G G T E D U K N O G E T R P A U
E R D L E P H A M A E R T S B S E M T N T R O C R
D O E B R G O P R S A I U N N P A G P E O R P P E
E B V B E G A L T G E U S T O R K P E E N R A O E
E A A E O R R R L O R Q G E O I V N G A E R A C O
R H E E T P A E P E S S O A N N I E Y C S H R F E
E T H Y P P H M A H R O N D B T E E S E R C S P P
```

SILLY SALLY'S SEARCH

Now that you're warmed up, let's turn up the difficulty. For the rest of the word searches, the words will still be found in adjacent letters in the grid, but not necessarily in straight lines. Rather, a single word may "snake" in different directions—up, down, left, and right—as you are spelling it out. Note that diagonally neighboring letters no longer count as adjacent.

Ready to start? Try to find all the alliterative phrases hidden in this grid!

Birthday Boy
Class Clown
Cookie Cutter
Crystal Clear
Dilly Dally
French Fries
Gas Guzzler
Gentle Giant
Heavy Hitter
Jumping Jacks
King Kong
Laundry List
Lily-Livered
Pet Peeve
Picture Perfect
Party Pooper
Rave Review
Road Rage
Temper Tantrum
Tongue Twisters
Topsy-Turvy
Treasure Trove
Vice Versa
Weeping Willow
Wishy-Washy

```
T P N N E E E P T Y N E R P Y Y D I O R S Y G O E
E E I K L E N P C R P A N H S W I N W L B E U R V
P E V E O P C L P T N T E A S L L E O L C R T H Y
R T U I K O O G R L A G E E R Y D A C S S C Y S T
E T C E L R U M E M R V E V U Y L L A N J A P O
C A C E Y T T L T A D I C R U R Y L O N P O C U Z
R L C O Y N W I R O A Y H H T U N G K G A W L R R
E E L J T A O S H Y W A S Y S K I I N B E D I L I
R A E H R E Z A E T Y Y R S Y E W C N A R I L Y E
P K V T S P M E T R V T K A G R V I T I E V N R W
T V R R T C E Y P P I T E C O R Y T L G E L S J U
T E A R U I P T O N C V R B O O I A D E N T T O I
R I P E I P A R O P E V A I R T R Y N G R R G O R
D R E W M I O N G G R A O B D H W W R R N T R I R
P R R F E E E Y N A E L Y Y A U R Y S T P R P C E
I P R T C T Y A E S Z Z P M I T C E L A C I H T T
V T W I S T E R T G U E I U J L O A C L A R E I H
U E T L A N O G U J I E N G C D W R A E S T A V Y
G N O T R Y V V Y A G E W G S N E T E A A J T S I L
R E U P E L J R T M V E J K Y V T O Y V L T D R Y
I Y N S A L U O E R T E A C V E E I W V G E N Y I
J P N U R E L O E T L W D T O W E F I E G P U A L
B E I I R T F S R L D P T N I P E R E N S E N F R
Y R S N O V A R R I W A P G W I L Y R C R I E T I
R O T V G E R E V I E D R G H E L O W H F R U P Y
```

REASONS TO LOSE YOUR JOB

WORD DIRECTION: SNAKING

Always late
Asleep on the job
Bribed client
Broke dress code
Drugs at work
Embezzlement
Falsified resume
Foolish tweets
Harassed coworkers
Hired by competitor
Inappropriate emails
Lavish business trips
Leaked company secrets
Laid off
Long bathroom breaks
Office gossip
Overindulged at happy hour
Poor performance
Porn at work
Quit
Refused boss's directions
Retirement
Sent inappropriate email
Slept with boss
Stole office supplies

```
P E P N H A S S O R A N I T D N R H L S A A I T O
E R E B I A P R P P P S E N O L S L I S H T W T S
L C D I R B Y I A T E L I G N S R D T I E N E E E
I R B R E D C P I S E M A B E L E K O L I B S C R
E E E O P M O P O S R H T A N Q O R O F T O D P F
N A U T E H C E G E O T R O L A W O C D E B S L F
T N R I T C I F B M O P U E N T Y R E K S S O G L
O T L R K A A F R N E K O N E Y F S O F M A S L E
E O I E O O M O E A N E H P M E O O T R O R S I S
I E S N U T G K S K O K Y W E L O E Z B H A E A F
S N E P P O I F T W O R P E Z Z M R A S V B I M U
E E N T L A P N A P I A P B C N A O A H E E W E L
P R A A L E O R N S P H R M E N P F S L M U E E T
O T L Y S P T T A T A T O V E R O R I A F S U Q A
U E O A L O W I D N D E G L N I O E F D R E I M I
S R L W A T E T H S T S O U D R R P I E I I T C R
I T A C D E P S B E E B F S S E T E L E N P R O P
E K O O M K I C O I E R P C E R I B R E A P O R A
C E E A P A R T S S E L G O R E I A E S F O N E F
R S Y N T E I U S I N A E D D M I Y A S S L D F U
E B O N T L G B H S I V A K E E N S N O S A I E S
T S P O H O R A S R D I L O R B T F O I S F D D B
L E E P E E W T G U S E P P U M I F E T W F O E O
S A I O J F O R I O I S E P S E C S L C U O O O S
H P I B R P I K A O R E P M B I H T O E R I D S S
```

1968

1968 was one of the most eventful years in American history. Here are just a few of the headlines, from across all 12 months. Can you find them snaking through the word search?

Auto Workers Strike in France

Chairman Mao Decrees: "Down to the Countryside!"

Chicago Hosts First Special Olympics

Chinese Actors Protest Yellowface

First Humans Ever Orbit the Moon

Gunman Kills Robert F. Kennedy

Hair Debuts on Broadway

Helen Keller Dies

Hispanic Students Walk Out to Protest Inequality

Hot Wheels Toy Cars Start Selling

MLK, Jr. Assassinated

Nixon Wins Election

Papal Statement Prohibits Contraception

Seventeen Casualties in Coast Guard Disaster

Single "Hey Jude" Goes On Sale

Students Protest Vietnam War

Swaziland, Mauritius, Equatorial Guinea Gain Independence

Tet Offensive Begins

Three Dead In Orangeburg Massacre

Yale Votes To Admit Women Students

```
R K N N U A D G D S N A U T O W O E I N F R A N L S C E T D
H I A M G O M S R M E N A I T K R K L A U Q E C T N L E G N
N L V O S T I T W O A S T U V E D I I T A T N S E T O M T R
F L E T E S Y F E E L S A D U R B R E Y M E I T O P R I T R
S S L A Y S D H C A E L R E T S S T E Y T E D T T C K T S N
B R O O W W E I C S U S A N T T S Q I S O S G U O H O T E K
I E B R E N N A A G T G S S S U D E N T S P D O T W N I N W
T R T F K E Z A D O H L T S D T O T L E T R U K E H N C W C
R U A M D L I W S S O Z R A S N W H S T S O A L E T N T O N
I T I U N A I F S T M P C R E T O E C V E T W S L I O V E S
C A L S T S R I A L Y I I B I H D T O I C Y O T S L S I B S
S S E E S P E C H O L C T T E O : S U E A O E N R C B S E N
I N O Q U A T G N E R S S R T R P E N T R Y D U T S C N G I
N G S H S T E E A T N O C E P T T E A M S S I D E N I E F F
E L E X I O G A T S T R A C A I N R A W S H I S P A E L T O
H G O O N R I R O Y T E U S N O E C R E T A R N A Q M T E G
E E W N I O A N Y I P A L S T E M E N I L S T O D G M A R D
Y D I E U G L T T W A P R C A T O D G A L E M O F R U S C T
J U N A G A J S T E A S Y A N M A A S A S I E K U E B S A A
A E S E C I T I A I P V C M R T O T T E R D H T T G N A R O
E L D N I N X L D R A A H A I P R E I T F D S E I T I F N N
C T E I D A R L C L H E T O R S T S N T G R E A B T C E D I
T O P T W O S N D S I E C A I O Y N A S U A O O R E R T A E
I T E S A R B C H I N E S E Y B E T O A R A E R I O F O D D
O N N Y N N O S R M C C E K L L S N O C N V E O D R T A E
N E D R A L R A T R V N A F W O I R S E S I E R S S H R E
W N C N R D E B U M D T U E L R F N T I T L S E T V E S S E
S C E A I S I N A T E D D R L E K E H U M A N B T E L O O A
S U T H O S A S S A R N I E S H N E L E L U S A F N T E N A
E U F L I C T T H O J K L M R S E H E A S Y A C N E E A E O
```

SOUNDS ABOUND

Swoosh! Plop! Brrring! Based on the clues, can you find the sounds in this word search?

Sound of (a):

banshee	cowboy	frying pan	parrot	something big landing in water
basketball net	distant	giggle	pig	something landing in water
bee	lightning	goose	race car	something disappearing
carbonated drink	dog	hesitation	rain	train
car revving	donkey	horse	sailor	villain
cash register	doorbell	hooves	santa	witch
cat	dry leaves	hostile animal	secret	wizard
clock	duck	lion	sheep	
cold	explosion	missed joke	silencing	
cow	fire	mud	sneeze	
	frog	owl	someone crying	

```
G O A W M L I K C A N O P S S T A I H T C H A U P
S U R O O O N I K C G D Z Z B R S A K E K E G L S
T L F O G L R H L E O G D U B E I P S L P R A H O
C E A S T R G R P E H N I Y H T T B N U M I W L Y
H O M H L M R K H R I R R T K T T E K H E B K H H
C O E H A Z E L P A A A U A A A P R L E O T A S H
H M C E E H A W T Q I S Q W S O O C W S W A H O B
O O C Y E S I Z A I A O C K H O H A H U A B R H H
H I I I W A L Z T P H E L H T O W O U S D W A Q W
E K I P H H E O B Z O Y B M H S I W Q T A I H Y A
H E H P E E H R R H L C R U O O U Q C S C A R B A
E U Z H G C O O R R O P I L M B H S I M S C H L O
K O W K I S H A A H P N L C U A K H A W Z H U E K
O R V Q E N H R H R A F O O B O H A H E O A W U W
O M C H O O Z A S S U U C P A H A B O U C T I R B
A S A O O O P L B I B Q H O N M O O A S E H W E I
O H A A B M S Z B O A U R O Q M U R D A C S H Z P
O H S W H F H Q D M C E E R S M K H L O A I R G O
K O H K H H I A H A K C H N L U W H I C S W A C O
S H O H R H H B M Z Z R L I S E O K T K C H G W H
H K P O C K I I I Z P H S L I E E C O T A I N G H
O M I E E E K T F I R K E E R S E R B O H C R A M
M E T A A H E E N U O W L K C A Z H H O H I O O O
N I D C I O T H E R L O O E S R C T R I O K H H K
K O C E U O H C E C S R G C T C S I B B O N O C R
```

KARAOKE

It's karaoke night! Below, you've been given snippets from the lyrics of 35 catchy tunes. Can you identify the song titles and find them in this word search?

"All my memories gather 'round her—miner's lady, stranger to blue water."

"A mulatto, an albino, a mosquito, my libido."

"Boy, was I a fool in school for cutting gym."

"Can you practice what you preach? Would you turn the other cheek?"

". . . Don't make it bad. Take a sad song and make it better."

"Far across the distance, and spaces between us, you have come to show you go on."

"Fish in the sea, you know how I feel. River running free, you know how I feel."

"Friday night and the lights are low, looking out for a place to go."

"Good times never seemed so good."

"If I could fall into the sky, do you think time would pass me by?"

"I'm not that chained-up little person still in love with you."

"I threw a wish in the well—don't ask me, I'll never tell."

"I've got so much honey the bees envy me—I've got a sweeter song than the birds in the trees."

"I've taken my bows and my curtain calls."

"Just a city boy, born and raised in South Detroit."

"Just call my name, I'll be there in a hurry, you don't have to worry."

"How high will the sycamore grow? If you cut it down, then you'll never know."

"I'm just a poor boy, nobody loves me."

"Laughing and a-running, hey, hey, skipping and a-jumping, in the misty morning fog with our hearts a thumpin' and you . . . "

"Now John at the bar is a friend of mine. He gets me my drinks for free."

"Now the half-time air was sweet perfume, while sergeants played a marching tune."

"Now Watergate does not bother me. Does your conscience bother you?"

"Risin' up, straight to the top. Had the guts, got the glory."

"Stacy, can't you see? You're just not the girl for me."

"Take my hand, take my whole life too."

"The colors of the rainbow, so pretty in the sky, are also on the faces of people going by."

"There's nothing that a hundred men or more could ever do."

"The world, for once, in perfect harmony with all its living things."

"Wendy, let me in, I wanna be your friend, I wanna guard your dreams and visions."

"We've got to hold on to what we've got—it doesn't make a difference if we make it or not."

"When I am down, and, oh, my soul, so weary—when troubles come, and my heart burdened be . . . "

"Yo no soy marinero, soy capitan."

"You are my fire. The one desire."

"Your love is like a shadow on me all of the time."

"Where troubles melt like lemondrops . . . "

```
R O L I N E E G O O E S I E M E T S S M O M T B B A M
A R H M E E Y M A R L K P U S S A C Y E A O W C A L B
C H W S L A B A N O A N A H M I M I E S D R Y Y N T A
T E E E A E M T E E R E U L E A R U O Y O S R T N U P
I N I I R I O H S W E K I L I L B W N E U F E E N O C
O O B T O P S N E E T I L S N E R O E Y O Y N L T W E
S N O O N O L E H T E R D O G E M H D D U P A C H O M
E L H O E V N T A S I E E O G F A L G A L U U L E H I
A I N T L O U N I I H H O V R O L R I A O C N O B E M
M M D N O M I H D D O W B I U S L E H O L T A V I N E
H E N U O H G H K N H L A V O N L H Y R S N A E R L K
V O A S A T M E N N H M N E B W I M T F O T O T T Y A
I W E T L T A N O U G E T H O I N I H H G I N C E E T
R A N U A T W T O R I T I A H E D W E T I M L A E A E
T I T O W A H N R O O O Y D M M B O A I N M L E I I A
T H A D O T O I V B E W N O L I N A N P G E Y B E L H
R E T D N O T M H A L S N S N A I M O I L M A P C F R
Y A W E M T S T N O E V I P R R A M I V U O N R A Y E
O W L R Y A T O P D I N E A H E E E H I N G O O E O L
R L U F N L G P B E L V E R T D I M R I L L M N A U E
I D M N C E S L R I M O U C N A C Y H W T Y E I P A I
T E I V L U O M M G Y E Q I T N I F E A R K C A N W N
R A S P I L Y E W H E R G N H E L O E V E R I E A O O
H E E O A N F O N A T I G E R M P W J O E E R W R E K
E H T F M O U T U F E F O E N D F N G L A M E M A T W
H L L I A P M P E R H T E Y O H A I I N E S N P H H S
C M A K E E A A C I E D U J Y E L L C U O P O I C E E
```

INFLUENCERS THROUGHOUT HISTORY

All of these (non-living) people made a significant impact on history. Can you find their full names in the word search grid below?

Ancient female mathematician

Ancient Chinese philosopher

Animator who created the first full-color animated feature film

Anti-apartheid activist

Bletchley Park codebreaker who helped shape computer science theory

Civil rights activist born in Alabama who fought segregation

Civil rights activist born in Georgia who fought segregation

Classical composer who couldn't hear his own works

Computer scientist who pioneered human-readable programming language

Famous diarist

First black MLB player

Former slave who helped many other slaves escape

Founding Father who authored the Declaration of Independence

Printing press inventor

Publisher of first computer program

First person in outer space

First woman Nobel winner

General who spent December 1777 at Valley Forge

Greek epic poet

Iconic 50s actress

Inventor of AC electrical supply system

Inventor of the first mass-produced car

The "Iron Lady"

Italian merchant who traveled the Silk Road

The last Inca emperor

Labor movement leader representing farmworkers

Outspoken (and longest-serving) First Lady

Microbiologist who made milk safer

Native American who helped the US explore its newly acquired territory

Nonviolent fighter for Indian independence

Nun who cared for the disenfranchised

Philosopher who promoted dialogue-based method

Oldest of three literary sisters

Renaissance man

Rock and roll singer with operatic range

Singer whose struggles with anorexia brought awareness to the disease

Teenage martyr of France

Theoretical physicist who predicted black-hole radiation

West Side Story star who won an Emmy, a Grammy, an Oscar, and a Tony Award

Writer and poet who explored themes around clinical depression

```
S V I K H N E F F E M A H O B A P A R I E V N R Y
Y L A A T S R I S J S M A T L F L M A T C I E U R
C N P L P O T S T M A L T M Z H A U H A U R R C W
N D R O C N E R H O W A D A G A N D I S E M E N S
Y F O N T E O N A G A M I S E E I H I D I D A T E
R T S F U N R N N Y R C H N T T R R A D B A V E C
N E U I C H E O M L I R C E U B M A H E R L O L A
O H O S N U N A M H I E E Y E O A M O R N N A N K
O T N D I I G O A F A R C A E N N E H F E F R A M
A E S A B O K J N O O G A G R O N R R A M R O Y O
E R R R E R M S A O A A R I S M A T I R A E O E I
T C C K I N G E N I C R U Y K R L A O T I N L U T
R J A M I A R T A O L I N U P A A E W S E C E K H
E H T O R C R A R C O A E M A S P G A A H C S A E
U C Z O H E I M C O P L R E I O R A C V L R A R R
M T A P E E M E O S N A R P L E E S A E Z S N E K
A R H P E R H O J N T U R G U S O N L D I C C N I
M G T T O N A H K I O N I N D L E A A V I N A G N
G A R E E N A L O G T O V E W I G R D E T N R J I
R T U G S H T G C N L H T N N A V D O R K E P R K
E E C H A E E O E I H N E E B O R R O E O S L E N
B N T N R L S L L I S O A I T O E L N R N T S S I
A G E O R O T A M G A W R J A S E E A A M E A P U
I N N V B E T E T E G E H Y P E V E G N A U R L O
K W A H N E H P S O R O R R M L T F R D E L A O M
```

STARTS AND ENDS

All of these words start and end with the same letter, like "MIRIAM" or "LEVEL."
Can you find them all, based on the clues given?

Abnormal growth

Adjust one's own appearance

Bubble

Caribou

Close by

Competitively fast vehicle

Copier company

Emotionally cleansing

Emotionally empty

Faithful

Go past some threshold

Head wreath

Hello, for example

In a stupor

Irish James

Koala's home

Kind of Madagascar flora

Least amount

Luanda is its capital

Meaningless filler

More spacious

Networking device

Another networking device

Not apt to go out of style

Not big nor small

Paper containing paper

Paper letting one in

Pasta shaped like rice

Playground game

Polish city

Pop singer Grande

Process that ends in acceptance

Reminder

Radio transmitter

Recently passed time frame

Resolute

Another word for resolute

Secret society

Shakespearean character

Symptom of a cold

Tag

Telling

Temporary problem

Tiny amount

Truffle, for example

Type of boat

Type of herb

Two under par

War-supporting, like an
aggressive bird

What's left

```
G L L T A I S D C S E V R O I A I L S Y O A A O R
A E K C R I A L E P F F E F S A O R L A L R E N O
E A O N A A N E O E E O F L T M O B M N O O G A I
N T R E U A I A E A N R F U Y I L D O G T I F I T
B E R E S A L I S M U S I T R E U S T G E O T C A
E S G E T R I T S D I M N E C A C X R L D N A U O
G R P N I I L S M I N C M A H T A B S R C I T T R
A S I G A B F C U R C I T R O R L E L E A C A E R
L E D N A W S H M R I I C M O H S T P L K O I B E
F R G O H K I I M P L E S E L E U M E T M T W I O
F I R Z S N A T A O L H S T L I A H K C O D I M L
S N O N M I M K L M E T O L U E F T C R A L C U S
L A P S L L U T P M I R P S O E I U M R A M A R L
S S R U I R R E I A E R T I S S C A R L E O X O S
T P F O K E E D N N Y U H C I A L A S R N R D O C
O X O Y A N M E D T E S U L T A N U M I O E Y G S
S T K A I A R M O E N L T A L O G B E T A X A D R
D A F D N M E Y P A N M H C N B A A D R R E S T E
E R M E R A O L O E S R O P A L B O I A N Y A A I
T E I N D N A H P T G T A S C O I R U I U A W O A
E R R E D Y I R D E Y A H N E T E G M A E F I M U
N C I U A T L D B A E I R I H C V L I H L U A O T
S K T E A M M A N E L F R O G N I A R C A R A W T
G E O P N E C M E S A L A A H L O C A T R S A W T
I T L E V Y S C R H U R E L R A C E H I D R U U L
```

ADD AN "I"

In each of these word pairs, an "I" has been added to spell a different word. For example, if the clue is "Story arc ⟶ Airplane driver," then the words PLOT and PILOT will both appear in the word search grid.

Angry → Cleaning person

Assume stance → Composure

Burn → Type of furniture

Celebrity → Step

Cook → Leader

Dishes → Exercises

Downpour → Gaudier

Exchange → Rant

Fighter → More rectangular

Green cartoon character → Scream

Guy → Primary

Join together → Brandish

Loud disk → Leaving

Most difficult → Most robust

Oscillate → Type of form

Redden → Unhealthily tinged

Resist → Worship

Respects → Daydreams

Robot → Mechanization

Shelled animal → Call dibs on

Small fastener → Hairstyle

Story arc → Airplane driver

Trick → Token

Type of cancer → Performance

Waterbird → Strong drug

```
A H E R O O S P S R P R B W E E I S R R E S T O M
O I S H I N E S E A O A D M B R V F H O T P U A A
C R N R E K R I I I E B I D H C M R H N A L H N T
N I B C S T I A D M U S S T A H H L A D P T E O I
I U L Y I X I P A M O A E D R H T A R E I I S R M
S D E F O D T E T O T U G O F L I E N S C L C A A
H H S O P U L M T N S S G N R E C I T H A L I R N
S R I E K R G A P A I R O M W C I R E R T T E S T
L E W S T X A C C E F A H A A H A V G B H H A T T
G R O H D E I I P K N I E T I D R F S O X R I G I
A H D W R R I T D E O T G C V E R M I E E R S N G
T E I A V E O F E T R E H B R O I F D E I R E I O
S H W R R L W A E D I I O F W S U L S Y F E R D X
W O L O A M T E O A P E E E H H A B T A I V E O T
I R M T D L C N C R O R C I A R E V E R E T L R S
E R S E T A M I O T S E E H C D R I R K E A I O B
E R I L A B E C T T T O T S E I S E E R R T I X N
L D W I P H H H E C T D E S T L R A D R R L E A A
I N A A L D U E F M A I I H P L I L R A F O R P E
R A M I C H C E E T O O T S K O T M D G A A R D I
R H I W V R C T E U S S A A M H O Y U B E D E L E
S O E L D P R T P S D E O O I R E O R A I C T W
N A S A L I D N N F E L N A E D W H E N A O A A R
I R L T O T C O N R A D I A L O G V A N X T R L R
E W W T D W A O H U V I D M R A E I W R M E M S N
```

ADD AN "L"

In each of these word pairs, an "L" has been added to spell a different word. For example, if the clue is "Cooking device ⟶ Story," then the words POT and PLOT will both appear in the word search grid.

After three → Baking ingredient

Aristocrat → Infinite

Barbaric → Saved property

Bubble → More skinny

Chose → Preserved

Clip → Location

Colonel name → Defames

Condemned → Organized

Drew in → Nursed

Digit → Someone who throws

Farm animal → Brag

Fire → Chat app

Indisposed → Crafty

Knife → Mess

Larger → Woo

Meals → Deluge

Nasty wound → Manner of speech

Pitter partner → Dish

Prefer → Taste

Programmer → More frigid

Ship → Swell

Smile sheepishly → Easier

Supporter → Darker

Vision → Minor

What you do with gas → Chubby

Wild hair → Type of folder

```
A U R G R G L M N D G I C L T I P O T L R U R A U
S E S C P R C O I S P S K C D P F A E F L O N U F
E E B E N I U M M E M N F O G E R G L N N I L P S
C A V N P E T C B R B T R U A U L C R A F L A N R
C P I O M C I E I A O A C L V T T G L I N S C D E
S I L P U A O F S L I S S A G F E R G S R E R E I
C G O T O U N N I I A C R C A L N P F N E D L L P
T H D T I O D S N C A P E K A B P T L S D C O I M
L L L L K O F N U O C C A E N C N G L S M N O S I
F A E E C A T T L T U L P E D T A O A C L L I T R
D F L E I L E S E T R A N N G K S L T K I N F C C
V C K D P K D S R E R O O T N S L E C T E O L E O
T U S V I C F C R N A V A M S M A M D C T L M E D
H G I T T A L F T A F F S O R K N V A R E S N R T
T S L E R S D P E K B S P E U N I A S I M L T L N
A G E E O P C M R C A F T T T A L O L A M I T C E
O L S R A L S A P B S A R E C K P B S T T F T E C
P C L S C E C N N E I L S L I U E F R E S R I U S
M U B A N C V D E O M L E R E A D A O G I S A C K
C L R O D L S L A E M A O T T T P T T N L C T D E
L P S R E N D I K R E M U E P A M R E I E T S S S
T S A V P A M N S U N D I T A P I C F L S S U O C
L O L A C E T A R I P K C R O L B C G E E T N O R
F O E G L S E M K C O C S I U L A R N R P N S I E
O D K E E T L N E D M P L N A F V O I F C G G M P
```

ADD AN "R"

WORD DIRECTION: SNAKING

In each of these word pairs, an "R" has been added to spell a different word. For example, if the clue is "Cooking device ⟶ Home for ships," then the words POT and PORT will both appear in the word search grid.

Believing → Entombing

Blackout → Indignation

Blistering → Woofing

Bowie 1975 hit → Painting holder

Celebration → Cheeky

Chess piece → Crustacean

Cook → Slow

Dress → Full-sized

Droplet → Money (slang)

Explosive noise → Sweeper

Fade away → *The Magic School Bus* Ms.

Fee → Bridge inhabitant

Going out → Moving quickly

Grandma's helper → Stretch

Money → Collide

Nintendo boss → Surfing tool

No more → Fear

Not lean → Like someone who likes to party

One of Pooh's friends → Bring about

Pale → Breakfast treat

Period → Expression

Squish → Swamp

Subject → 23°26′ north or south

Symbols of merit → Annoys

Touch → Agreement

Underground place → Sculpt

Water source → Young plant

```
E O G E R P A T A B T S T A B A I N G B R O E H D
E W N T A T S A T Y E H R N T R K G P O R O B G L
E A O M Z Y O B I P O P A S E C I E L L T M R G T
P T N R B A U T G E E I G N C R O S C A V K A R L
O U O A R T O R A M S L R Z B O P R A W E P W W S
D O S K B I R E A R F L A P Y T I F M O L R P P B
D R P E G E B R D I T O O A G R C Y E D C G A D C
G I T S W A M A M Z Z S U T E N T E S B R A S G O
G A S H C P N F E D L E G F L Y G O A E A F H Y I
E R S S U E S R H E P T D A N I T D C T T A T T A
O N C T C I D A B R R I K B G H R A E Y T W A R F
C T A C E P G E R S B I R B O B A D D D R D C P M
A D E A N O R A E W A G E S W D D A P S E A W E W
P R T C D A T B R P Y F C T H A Y T O S O T E A E
R T B E A M A B S A B A O N S B D G U T B W C P A
F B O E N H S U M S I S H O A R E R C A A E A N C
O U E T K E D R A H L A I F R V U U A P P B I N N
S A S L D S E Y R S E R Y O A R N A F F S N F E D
Y R F A R A W I N G K A E L K C U Y I U L E G M V
Z T T L P I N G G F R B E A R O B U N G C A E T T
A S R W E A G B A F L D T C N C R E G V R G R O
P E N W A P N I K S T G R I G G V A N O E C S H W
R R P O E G N U E L Z A T B U E R N E T Z C A S N
S E B T I N G N N R Z I F O O M Z E S E R B O R I
W O R F T A P I T A D O T E R R P H A N G B A O R
```

COMPOUND WORDS

In this word search, the phrases given are hints toward the compound words hidden in the grid. For example, "Atmosphere art" is a clue for the word "Aircraft," since "atmosphere" is a synonym for "air," and "art" is a synonym for "craft." Can you discover all of the compound words in the word search grid?

Atmosphere art
Awesome innate
Concise incident
Corpse protect
Dance viewed
Dark committee
Disk seat
Flame labors
Foal energy
Foundation globe
Lawn jumper
Message novel
Noggin delicate
Planet wriggle
Powder skillet
Reverse terrain
Ringer tush
Shake meander
Sketch connect
Sugary core
Sweetie brush
Twenty-four hour
hallucination
Verify friend
Weapon hole
Woman nag

```
O L M G K A G E R O C B W C H A L T W A L A Y D D
I L T T E N S K B O W H H L O I R D N A T D M R A
D R A L E S E S L R M T E E C N R C A R R K R E A
G B L A O N A W K O N R A C R S R A A T E L O A M
S M E E T K S T A T U M E N R F A N R E O F B O N
G D T B O O U R N E R E C L A A I C C A O C M R S
S U N D R D P E D G A L R E R H S S A B O G E L H
T P A A A W B R I B A R U P P O J I R E T A O E G
W E M P P M R A N U C A A A R E Y R G L A M K U M
L R T I I T H N D R K R Y R M R D R A L N B I A E
Y E A T D W A U O R G P A E D T P H O K R B N H A
R W B B H O K P R H O T E S G E O E B K C A S R A
A R Y A O R T E G M A L T W A A O S P L A C F E I
L A E S R T E E G B D E A S S R I K E B L A S E R
E O P E W S T R C L R R M D R O H R L A E L O E B
D W D E E A R R E E T I L R C D R O R I F L A T R
D E R T H K M E R F H G D B E C T W E M O A R A K
W B D A K B L N R R T W A E A I B K F T D B R R E
E E L T O I G U S K R O H H U D H R A C S E H Y D
U G L B J O Y B R U L W F B D U E R R T T S A A W
D S N O G E D A M A P L G B O A I R C B O N B S E
M E W T E H C L E C B T A A D O T K H A H E A G A
N O L T C K T E S B M D W D Y A O H D A C Y G I O
B S K O K M A R S E K R A U G L S F B M O N T J E
A A E M E A I O F D R A B K N R E W U D R R H R A
```

COUNTRIES OF AFRICA

For the final word searches, you're really on your own: there's no list of clues to help you out. Can you find the 54 countries of Africa hidden in this word search?

```
E U E E A N G R P U B F T E N A S H T U O S A I N
E R D R R A H R E B L O H E C D U J D R O M A A A
V U D O C T I C T O I C I C I T B I Y A Z T A N Z
E D E M I S U N O A S U H O N U O R U M Q U E A U
P O G N E N N E M E A P T X G O R U B B I L E R I
A C A R R T A E A D N G O S E D P N D P I A G E O
A P L E O P Y G R P A N L A L A I N I O E B C P E
E I A E N O F O I N P E U Y O A R E G I Q O N U B
I T I N G E R A A C I L M N A G A M E H C A I I L
R A N E K G D E Y N S G I I M M B B E T T F O C E
U A K B N I M A F E K R W A N I A I O O H A N N A
A M A B A B B N D A N M A A D Z B R G C E W A A C
Q E E R T I A N U S F A I R E S W E N O O S T K O
U O R I I C N A I D A D G A L S L R I A O B O U R
A T Q A R E E P L A G A S C L E L E R B A P N R A
B I A L G B C C S M E N E S E Y I B N G A U O S H
M S O R U I N U S O A L S A H C I I R G B T H A C
A A M O O G E A W T M I T O C O V I B N I I R F I
Z G C C T O L R I N L A N O Y R A W B L F C I A Z
O S O A I S U L A Y O S T E M A L A U I C A S W I
R M D A R E I R U V B I U N I S O S P C I D N A L
O A A H L G T I A M A N G M A I A A E A R F J C E
M E N C A B U N U I C E A E C V A F R N O A R T N
O C I U G S O S A S S I B R O O N D E R O L A A K
B Z A E O G A L I B Y A B U R K I W N U G A N D C
```

ELEMENTS OF THE PERIODIC TABLE

50 of the best-known elements of the periodic table are hiding in this word search. Can you find them?

```
C R O F Z Y I O R N I T A L P E L M I A I T I O C
B I U L U G C I S U M N C T C C I D N M R P I R H
N N I U U I I U B U R M S M I Z N O L M Y R M O M
B E R E M U T O R E U A E C N S E L E R C U M U I
O C U P R I O U E S I L N O A R I N M U U N Y I R
N I I R A M N M N A G M I N D O N D N H T I O S M
G N Z C B U M U I N N A X E A R O I R E R L D I U
I S S O N I N O H I M T N U U I C L S U R C P T O
M L G F D C K E I L U M U I M E R A C M L I Y R N
E A D R S C O L N A I U B R O N M N E U M E N K I
L L I U M O P S S O M D Y O M I A G S I N H U M M
A M U I A T R R T M C A H H B R O R N O S E K Z I
P R O S S A I L E I P A L Y O G L O N E E G P N N
U N F I O I A R A N I I S D R E H N N O L L N O S
E I U L D I A T D M U I L S I N C I R N M O M G G
E T M A C N E U I M L S I A L R A U S U U I N R E
A M U U R N M M I R A R C I V O R D I S I H O A N
U E C F L E I N N S C B O N E O S I A P N O R T I
G R C S U G O R U I O N N N R E E N D T A B U R O
A I C I U Y X A N C I H C S U B I L G I T D I I G
M P H O M U I R I U M N C I L D C A I C O M O R E
U R E S G O R T T Y U K R D E A P X N P P N N O N
S O H P M L U C O B A L T S E L E M M E R C I H U
O M F Y M D G L I I U M U I R O N I D S G P C E L
I I A E I I I E T H C I O I M R M U B T M A M U I
```

THE HUMAN BODY

There are 50 parts (or systems) of the human body hidden in the word search. How many can you find?

```
N Y M I P H A G U S C N A P A N E R N A T L E U C
L A M N O S R A A I R C A L F F S E D I L C A O L
Y S U A D E O T N I E M L C P C N G U N P P R W I
S E N E T T M R E P A T D R R S I S K C T S I V A
T E M Y S Y S T E C S Y E T S Y F E S O T N E I U
A B A V E K A W M U N E A E R R E T R U T E Y E C
L O O I T O X N C E R U N R U F S U A B A L E F S
E L L N S H Y L H E U M S D M E S H R L S H L X N
A R T S E D C C L E K A I N N A N L U H S E A R Y
V E E B G I C O C E B R A Y B U O B E H L O K F B
U E A R N X N Y R A H K P L L T T L R I F S H F C
C U O B R N R M A D P N T C E D O N T L R V E R A
I T D S D V E H E P A E H H B M P H S O M I H D N
S O O F E O U E O A R R C E S Y L P E N E L A N O
T E L T T S E R A S T R A A T A Y E L S K E L E T
N E P F A G F O R R A S E M R N R I V P L C O N O
H E S B D V K L E Y E H R T N A D S A P E M L R B
N L E C A A N E A M S N E D L S A M S C G V L A T
E O I W L A H H D L G L A D S E C A S A E S N E N
S K G S Y A P A F U N B I M X N B F B P I L L M O
E S L E D I H R B A L L N D I T L C C A M R A B D
M O B K E H G A S G P P E C X N A D D C H Y B A V
M W N C A N M S E R A M E T I R C H E R D O Y O W
A T U O B A E I N T N I Y S C S U L A A M A C H D
L H T M T R H T S E T N S Y R O T A N A O T S Y S
```

COLORS

In this word search, there are 60 color names hidden in the grid. Can you find them all?
Note: This puzzle includes one-word colors only.

```
O Y R H C U F C U L S U S M O L E C E H C A E V I
T O Q S I Y R H M U G T C M Y D U L N I R A P O L
A R I E A T R E L L P E A C E N U B B U A M Y R R
I L L N R N S E B R O L R E R U G R U Q A Y T N Z
L Y E A R E G I W A A A I T E L R A O D C A I U M
T H O G R E E M E H T W H S O E U S V E L F R R E
N A R A Y U W R A Y E M O E R A N T I E E O C O A
L M O N Y R N G C U V R G A M N A U O U R A H C L
E A L E I A U A H A M N I I B R N A T E E R A R T
Z A A P R B B R E U I N D R E A Z I G S A N A M L
U H B L A S U T R S E E N I R E P E A I E N C R B
D A Z S A B R O P O C L K W I E Y G R O D R A R V
A U S T L N N T A R M C T E N I E N A R I O L E L
R M S A R G E L L A U A A G T A L D W M N I V T E
E D I A D S H L M O N N O A W O L O R E A D L O T
I S L R C G S A L R R E E M S E A L O W L O L G A
L V E R E G P M F W A R I L E T T F N I R E A M L
T U P A C G O H E F Y K L A W T N A R O C N L D S
Q R O T L M R I R W N C O C R Y O V Y W E N A R E
U T Y R T I L W G O B L A L P Q S Y D A M I L H M
O P U R E R L E D R Y I C C O R E A M S E C R E E
I A Z S M C E U M B U U K I T H S J E E A N E D I
S E A O I R L B A R I A P R L T A E A D C Y A N E
E T B N I V O M O O M E E L P B A Z J I R E N A V
N L D L T Y R C N S N E C A R R O N E S E C L L R
```

WILD ANIMALS

There are 60 wild animals hidden in this word search (each is 6+ letters long). Can you find them all?

```
B T N A H P E L R L A N A L O D O K C P E I S H L
O H A P I U G E E L E T H P H K E L O C A F Y L L
A T T N N E N P P O R N I Y S C R I D W P M U A E
N N Y P E P E Z H R R A A B A U O C O O P A S W J
N A O W A R L A I R O N O O B A N A M P O T W N F
M R O R A E L G L B R P O S O T E O N P I H T E A
A K O M O D R A C A T K E T E E L U R C W N E F T
D I R O D O T G P R H A N R I C E M A H O L A F F
L L L N T R N O L A T E S R E H U J U P E F F U U
O O G G O I N A D O T L L R K C E A G S O R A E B
T H M W I H A E C E R T W O O D P A K C I I G L A
R H C E S E U G I H S G R N R T S T R I O R P O R
A I U S A V E R N T G M T O A G N O E C T T H O B
W D P B E R C U A H S A L M E K A C E M P Y A N E
F N O T C O I P P R C H P A E M O E A L L E T R A
L A A G O P W I N E I I M N Z S B Y B E A N I M O
A M I N E S C T E R N E R H C A O P A B W E R Y N
A E A F S P L I W W D E E N A N O I E S R V C E K
T T N A I O A D A L R U S A I H R L A O N L H E E
E R A T P P T Y S T R K R C N I N O E D W O H A T
O N G U O R G P U V A E L I O C E O M R A L L I G
R A L L K A O R R D S P E A A N R C C A P O E L A
C O Y B S L L I A Y A L W S R W O F C L A A O O T
S A O P B O A N A R E A M E G H S N O A F R W R O
A E T A C B I E T E D N A L L A E I S N E N N A T
```

FOODS

There are 60 foods hidden in this word search (each is 6+ letters long). Can you find them all?

```
L P A I C K B R Y R E G N A R O A C C G L N O A H
A N T N A L E R A U R W A R R N S N H I I L P O O
O N D G E B E M A H E T C T O R S E K C N G M S N
M L S G T N P B U R G L E A A T P R O L E D U L A
L A H P L A R I O L E E T A L Y I M A N E W O E R
O E C I A T O C N A M R E W A R R L E A R Q L F I
O Y T W D B Y I R P S T T P E N E D Z T E C A U L
G U R D N N I S A D L E L E L P B L E P R O B E R
T N Z S A I U E L I S M E R U S A R K E E L S T I
O A U C C H Q T L A A O O R B A N C A P N A B W O
S S S E T S A L P K I N T I T P M U F F I N E A R
H O I T R P W N M I C A C H R N I E N A G H R R T
B R C S I E T U U L A F A I A I S H C P S E I Y S
S L E E N E A T P A F S T O A G L I Q N N T T E N
C U S L G R O L H L E I P U S E A D A E T P P A I
N A M O A L S L T E A P P A S H S W I T A L C B P
K C U R E L M A E E I E L U M E M T O E Y E H E E
U A C E E D A M E E N P I E F O L I T R R R A E S
G L B T L L B E R C W O K E R C C A S F B E B S H
A P A O N N U I T T B R A T Y R O R B C E U L G R
N A N N E F R E U A R I C S Y R T A E M A A P M I
T Q U I R E P R A S S N P U O E B A L L Y E K R U
L A G N R M A K S E B E E C U B N C O W U T L P T
A S N A P G R R T N U A W A R S A R L O A L A O Y
T U N A E U L A U R H L E M T H M A L M E M T T R
```

US NATIONAL PARKS

WORD DIRECTION: SNAKING

There are 61 National Parks from across the US hidden in this word search. Can you find them all?

```
A A C A N O R E L E C S A L S I N I S N Y A C N R A H O T
I S C A Y O N Z N R A D N R T E C G S D N A H I E H A K S
B E N Y S N L I O L S D C A Y C A R I N N E J E F S A O P
H Y L H E B A S A C B A E V R N N K V A L L O L S G N I R
E D A S Q H N D A S V L R O B O Y N O A S I S H U K C A L
S B I O U A B E C A L S N M E S O E T O L L E Y A C A N B
E A L A E L G N D S S N I I H L N Y S W A L E R T L C Y O
Y H A K A V I B D S E T A T E N G S G A V W A R A T S E N
E D O S P A D S A E N N U O E A U C O D N I D S P F O R O
L N E H G L E S K O V N I M E D A U H C A B U K E D E T F
L A N E R C M O L L C A C N P U L Y A I V O K V T R I H E
A K K V C I P M Y E L T N I P N A P L M E L L A T I F A G
V A E E S E A S E V B A Y B I N C Y R U Y E L G G R H N U
H T D E E R O O A V R E I R S E L O S E V O A E R A N N I
O E S M R E R O S E R C C A L G D U N G A Y C I D N O O S
N A Y E A O A D E M D A A R C S A N E S H O S M C A N N C
L C T I G E E O A T E P T E A A S A R A L C R E D A Y I I
O V C O N T H N I N U I R R K E T I K N K E G R W N O E N
I I K E L A E F E L O T M L A N D D N A A L N A O S D K A
A W A H S T R L E R M Y K B L D S N I S S L A D O B R O I
I N T M M L G U A E I O C G E A T O G R T E R R O I G J F
C H E A O M D E N A L R N S Y B E T I L E S R R E T A N R
R A S I K K I N S N N Y O A G S I D A S M E D A W A Y M W
E N D E Y M A G S C A N S O R A N N B O O U A H C R A A L
G R R Y U O C A D I A R A M E B G A R G T N C L Y R M M C
O E T S N T R E T R E S E I A T C N I A R A S C T D O O U
G A R N I A O L I E T O R L O T I R N S H C S A O H T D R
S T D U S E Y S I M A F N E R C E E I A T N D G R C A V E
A N D N E L A A I N G T H E A O R A U G R O E U T W U N H
```

SUDOKUS

The first World Sudoku Championship was held in Lucca, Italy, in March 2006, with 85 participants. The winner was Jana Tylová, an accountant from the Czech Republic. Her advice? "Practice every day" and find example games online. The competition has been held annually, with 30 countries officially participating as members of the World Puzzle Federation.

The fastest competitors can often solve a booklet of 10 puzzles in around 20 minutes, averaging 2 minutes per puzzle. In fact, there is a round of the competition in which participants attempt to beat the Guinness World Record for fastest solve time on a "Very Easy" puzzle. Thomas Snyder, a scientist from the US, currently holds the record: just 1 minute, 24 seconds.

Sharpen your pencil: How quickly can you solve each of these?

WARM-UP

2	6	4	7	1	3	5	8	9
1	7	8	5	6	9	4	3	2
3	5	9	8	2	4	1	7	6
5	8	6	2	3	7	9	1	4
9	4	1	6	8	5	7	2	
7	2	3	4	9	1	5	6	8
4	1	2	9	7	8	6	5	3
6	3	5	1	4	2	8	9	7
8	9	7	3	5	6	2	4	1

135

4	3	7	9	1	6	2	8	5
2	6	1	5	8	4	9	3	7
5	9	8	3	2	7	4	1	6
8	4	6	1	9	2	7	5	3
1	5	9	7	3	8	6	4	2
3	7	2	4	6	5	8	9	1
9	8	5	2	7	1	3	6	4
7	1	3	6	4	9	5	2	8
6	2	4	8	5	3	1	7	9

235

5	**9**	**8**	**7**	**2**	1	**3**	4	6
4	1	3	**6**	**8**	9	**7**	**2**	**5**
2	**7**	**6**	4	**5**	3	1	8	**9**
7	6		**5**			8	**1**	
	2						5	
		5					6	7
	5	7	2		4	**6**	**3**	**8**
			8			5	7	
6	8		3	**7**	**5**		**9**	1

Now that you're warmed up, let's tackle some more challenging sudoku puzzles. If you can solve one of these in less than an hour, you're doing great!

	8		9	7	3	3	1	
7	9	3						8
		1	2	8		3	9	
	5		7			1		3
		4				7		
3		6			8		2	
	6	9			7	2		
	3					9		1
	1				9		3	

	5					4		
8			3		2		1	5
		4		5	7			3
9	1							
	4		2		9		3	
							4	2
4			1	7		3		
3	2		5		4			6
		6					5	

				6	9	7		
		2	8	4			6	
6	9		5			8		
	1				3	6		9
7		8	1				5	
		1			2		3	7
	2			3	4	1		
		3	6	1				

	7	8	5					
1	3	6		7	8			5
		2			1			
5	9			8				
8								3
				9			8	2
			8			5		
3			7	1		8	6	9
					6	3	4	

	6		8		5			2
8	1					5		
2				6	3	9		
					2		3	8
			6		1			
6	4		9					
		2	1	8				9
		7					5	6
1			5		7		2	

				1			4	
1	3				2			6
		5			6	2		
	9		2	8				7
	8		7		3		9	
5				4	9		8	
		4	6			5		
7			9				1	8
	2			5				

7		6			8			
3	9	4			7			
			2			6		3
9			1					5
	7		9		5		2	
4					2			8
5		9			1			
			8			1	4	7
			4			5		9

AN ELEMENT OF FUN

If you've made it this far through the sudoku section, you deserve a break! The next five puzzles, themed after the five natural elements of antiquity, offer some quirky twists on the traditional sudoku structure.

LIGNUM

Letters instead of numbers? Why not? When you solve this sudoku, you'll have a letter of the alphabet in each cell, from a set of nine distinct letters. Use the clues to decipher the letters that are represented by symbols.

CLUES

- comes after
- alphabetically
- spells the full name of a
- nth
- is a one-letter chemical element symbol, as is
- The nine symbols each represent a different letter

		S				A	R	
			A					
	J		M					
J	E		Y					
S								J
	A				O			S
			M			C		
				R	A			
	J	E				Y		M

TERRA

Each caterpillar in this sudoku puzzle is crawling between two pairs of consecutive numbers; for example, if a caterpillar's tail is at 8, then its head is at either a 7 or a 9. Good luck filling in all the cells!

		7						
	9			1		5		
			8			4	9	
5						2		
3		8	5		2	7		1
				3				5
8		3	9				7	
	4		7					
7				4		5		

AQUA

Here's another one with letters instead of numbers.
Unscramble the letters in the boxes with circles to answer the clue below.

 → MOVE IN A STREAM

	L		K			T	BODY OF WATER	R
A				E				W
		A						
K								F
	E				W	K		
F	T			L				
	COULD DESCRIBE WATER PRESSURE			K		T		
	A		O					

90   Only the Hardest Puzzles

IGNIS

In Mrs. Molecule's chemistry class, you need to be very careful about which substances you mix together! There are nine types of labeled vials available, but to trigger the right REACTIONS, it's important not to put two vials of the same kind in the same row, column, or three-by-three square. Once the vials are arranged correctly, what substance will you end up with?

__ __ __ __ __ __ __ __ __

					A		R	
O	A						T	
				S	R	A		E
E				O	N	R		T
			A		I			
C		N	R	E				O
N		I	S	C				
	C						O	N
	O		N					

METTALUM

In this sudoku, we've decided to help you out by investigating the six silver patches of contiguous cells marked in the grid below. Within each patch, you are provided with the sum of the numbers inside the patch. The other rules for completing the sudoku remain the same as usual. With your logic skills and a bit of math, can you fill out the entire grid?

6	2		7		1	=18		
	=17		2		6	1		
			=14					=19
		6		1		9		
9	5		4		8		2	
=10		4		6		5		
						=16		
7		8	5		4			
5			6		7		9	

HARD-CORE

		1			9			3
6	5			7	3			
				1			6	7
3					5			2
	6	4				3	9	
2			6					4
1	2			8				
			1	9			2	6
7			3			1		

8				4			5	
1		2	7		9			
						2	9	3
3						5	2	4
		5				9		
7	2	9						8
2	7	4						
			1		7	6		2
	1			8				9

				3	7		4	1
		7			8	5		
3			6	1				
2							3	6
7		6				1		2
1	8							9
				9	4			7
		1	8			9		
4	9		7	6				

		4		9	7			
7	3							6
1					8	4	7	2
		3		7			8	
			1		5			
	7			3		6		
8	4	6	5					3
2							6	8
			7	8		5		

8					6	4		
		1			3	5		
	6				7			
			4	6			7	2
9	7	2				6	5	4
4	3			5	2			
			6				8	
		9	3			7		
		5	1					3

		5	7					4
1	3				9	7		
				3		2		5
			1			3		7
6		3				8		9
2		7			5			
3		1		4				
		2	9				4	3
7					3	5		

		6		8				
	8		4	5	3		7	
3					6	4		
	2		9	1				
1		5		3		7		9
				7	5		2	
		3	5					7
	7		3	6	8		9	
				2		8		

CALCUDOKUS

The Calcudoku puzzle genre, invented by math teacher Tetsuya Miyamoto, challenges the solver to find numbers that add, multiply, subtract, or divide to produce a "target number." As you can see in the following example, the grid is divided into a number of *cages*, each outlined in dark black.

Your mission is to fill the grid, one digit per cell, so that the digits in each cage are mathematically combined to produce the target number for that cell. For instance, in the top right cage of this example Calcudoku, you are looking for three numbers that multiply to a product of 60.

An additional constraint is that, for an *NxN*-sized Calcudoku puzzle, the numbers 1 through *N* are each used exactly once per row and per column—similar to the rows and columns of a sudoku puzzle. (However, unlike in a sudoku, it's okay for a digit to be repeated within a Calcudoku cage.) The solution to this example is shown to the right.

×180		×126	+24				**3**	**5**
8					×72			**1**
×42			+11			**8**	+27	
×42		-2		×216				
		8	+21					
×15		**4**			×420		-3	
+17		**3**	×6			×35		
		-2				×504		
+24				+28			×21	

WARM-UP

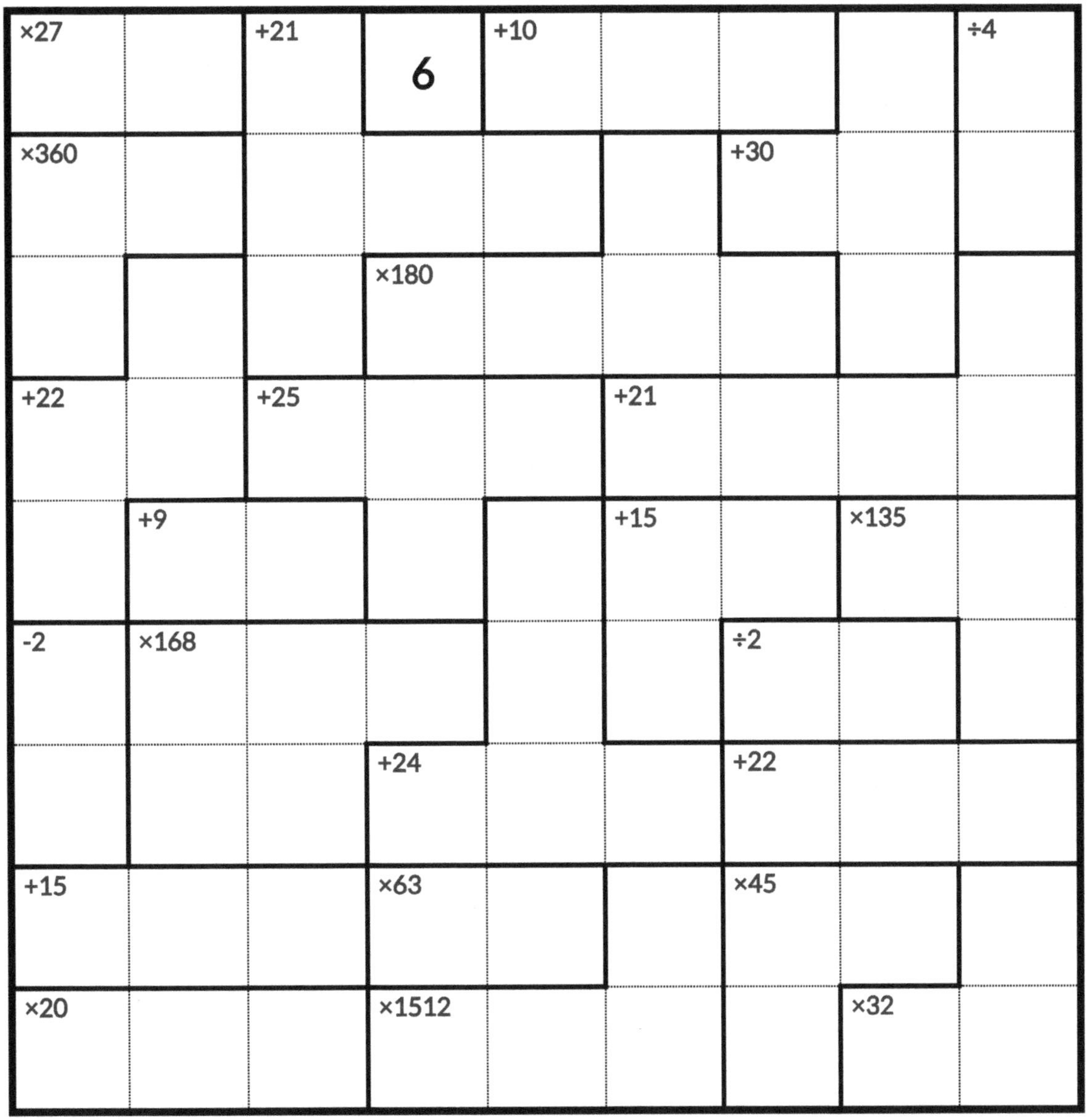
×27
+21
6
+10
÷4
×360
+30
×180
+22
+25
+21
+9
+15
×135
-2
×168
÷2
+24
+22
+15
×63
×45
×20
×1512
×32

+17	+13		+18			×162		
					×189		×56	
	+18			3		-3		
+20			+24		-4		+14	
×378					×48			
×864			+15	9	+13			
		7		2		+13		8
3						×315		
+26				+20			×24	

-3		+22				+12		
+27						+18		×280
	9	×648		5	3			
		4		+9			9	
+17		×252			+21			1
	5					+28		
	4	×1620		1	8		÷3	
-1				-1			5	×36
+20				3	×96		2	

×2160		×80		×63			+7	
			3	+16				×960
+19			+8			×144		
1			×504					
4	**2**	+21			+23			
+20			×128			+25		
×10		**9**		+22				÷2
			+18				**3**	
+27				+16			×18	

+12		+23			+15			×864
	×4320	**7**	×32					
8				**7**	+20			
-5			×1120					
×108	+12							**5**
	×336		×1215		+29			
	4			×10				**6**
+12		**1**	+17			×112		
+14		×32		×162				

×28		+25		×720		**1**		**6**
	5					+24		
3	**9**	×10	-6			×1260	+27	
7				**4**				
×60		×144					**3**	**9**
×864				×864			-1	
		×3780				+9		×35
+24					×360			
			×1728					

×11340 ×30 ×96 **8** **7**

×3888

4 ×24 **2** **5** +17

×84 ×1512 **1**

2 -2 +12 +11

×144 ×504 **1**

+19 ×1728

-4 -5 **8** **7**

+23 ×84 ×270

×280			×72				+8	
+28		+17		+30				
						-4		**6**
			+31			×180		
×12		-1		+24				+11
+22			×1440				**2**	
					5		**7**	
×360	+25		+22		**7**	**8**	-1	
					-1		×48	

TOUGH

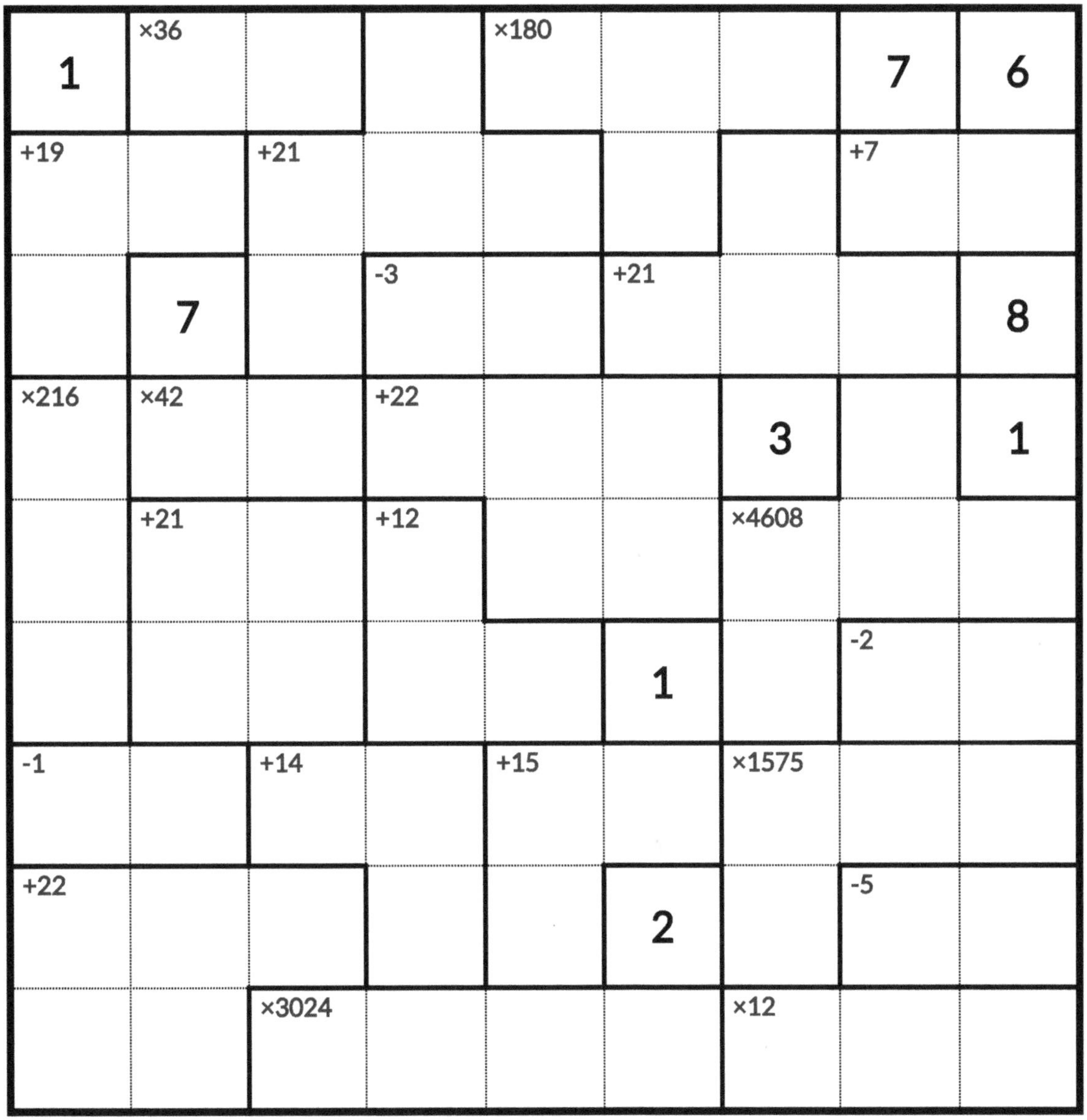
1
×36
×180
7
6
+19
+21
+7
7
-3
+21
8
×216
×42
+22
3
1
+21
+12
×4608
1
-2
-1
+14
+15
×1575
+22
2
-5
×3024
×12

7	9	+22		×1680		×405	
×32	+16						
		+14				6	
	÷6		×3402			×120	
2	+12		×9	+34			
+18	5	×392				-1	
		+7		8	+9		
+23		+19			×28		
	6	9	×12		1	×56	

-2		×378			×5		+25	
3	**8**		×360				**7**	
-1		×360				×108		
×35				×1152				
×36		+12			+20			
×36				×112				
	×5040				+17		+14	
8	**1**		×6				-1	
+25				×6048				**2**

×54		×70		+26		**1**	+16	
			×2160			**8**		**4**
×2520	**1**	**3**			**7**	+13		**2**
		8		+6			÷9	
	×360			×420			÷8	
	+22				×756			
+17	×4			**5**	**3**		**9**	**8**
	×648			**8**			×42	
	6			+21			**5**	

	+14	+25		1	+16		×96	
8				1				
5								1
9	×48		8	+18			×4480	
×864			+14					
7	2			+17			1	
+8			4		+27			
	×294			×32			+22	
×24		+19			1	×63		
	-3		×216				7	3

+9			+25		×12		+17	
+11	×126		×40			×144		
				5				
+16		×12		+22		×252		
	-4		×28				×40	
+11	+30		×288				×45	
					×280			
-1		+19						**2**
÷8		+24				+12		**9**

+19		**8**	×12			+26		**5**
	1	**5**	**2**		**8**		×2352	
×15		+13						
		-6		**6**	+5	×4320		**1**
+20		+26	**6**					-4
×5					+14		**2**	
+28		×2520			÷5		+15	
				+6		**7**		
9	×48		+13			+8		

-3	×288			+21				9
	4		×63			×90		
+22	6			+25			+17	
			+11			+19		
+18		+18						
	1			×315		×96		
7	9	×480						
1	7				×162			×20
×1008				-2		+23		

+11		**9**	×40		**2**	×84		
	÷9		+30				+23	
4		+18			×324			
9	×320					×1344		
		5	+8					×60
+20	×28		×2592			+18		
	×224			-1		+27		
2		-3		+8				**8**

-4		×56			-5		×2160	
								3
-5		÷3		×32				
						9		
×40			+16			-2		
					9			
+11		+14			×35			
	8		+16			+9		**7**
×84					×2160			×40
		3						
1			×2160				**7**	
		6						
-7							×16	
						7		
×9720			+21					

×6		**9**	+26					**5**
+32			**8**	×5		+23		
	7			+13				
	×2880				**8**		÷3	
9		**7**	-4		×1728		+20	
+8		**5**		+9				
3	×60			+16		+8		**8**
8		-2		**3**	×45		**9**	
+15		×6			×1176			

+15			×1296		9		+14	
×864					×200		×7560	
			×21					
+20			×120	×28		-1		
+15		9		7		2	×72	
				×96				×126
					×42			
+26		×450		1		+26		
6	+9		+19					

In a Kakuro puzzle, you are faced with a blank grid like the following:

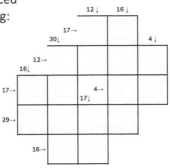

Your goal is to fill each cell with a digit from 1 through 9. For each horizontal or vertical line of consecutive cells, you are given the sum of the digits in that line. Also, no digit is repeated within the same line. In this example, for instance, you know that the two cells in the bottom row add up to 16.

This means that possible values for those two cells include either 7 and 9, or the reverse (9 and 7). Note that 8 and 8 would be impossible, since this would require repeating the same digit twice. And 6 and 10 would also be impossible, since all entries must be a single digit.

When fully solved, the grid will look something like this:

	12 ↓	16 ↓		
17→	9	8		4 ↓
30↓ 12→	6	3	2	1
16↓ 17→	9	8	4→ 17↓	1	3
29→	7	9	8	5
16→	7	9		

In some cases, there will be multiple disjointed lines of cells in the same row or column; in these situations, it's okay to repeat a digit in the same column, as long as it isn't repeated within a contiguous line. For instance, in the middle column of this example, you can see that the digit 9 appears both in the top cell and the bottom one.

WARM-UP

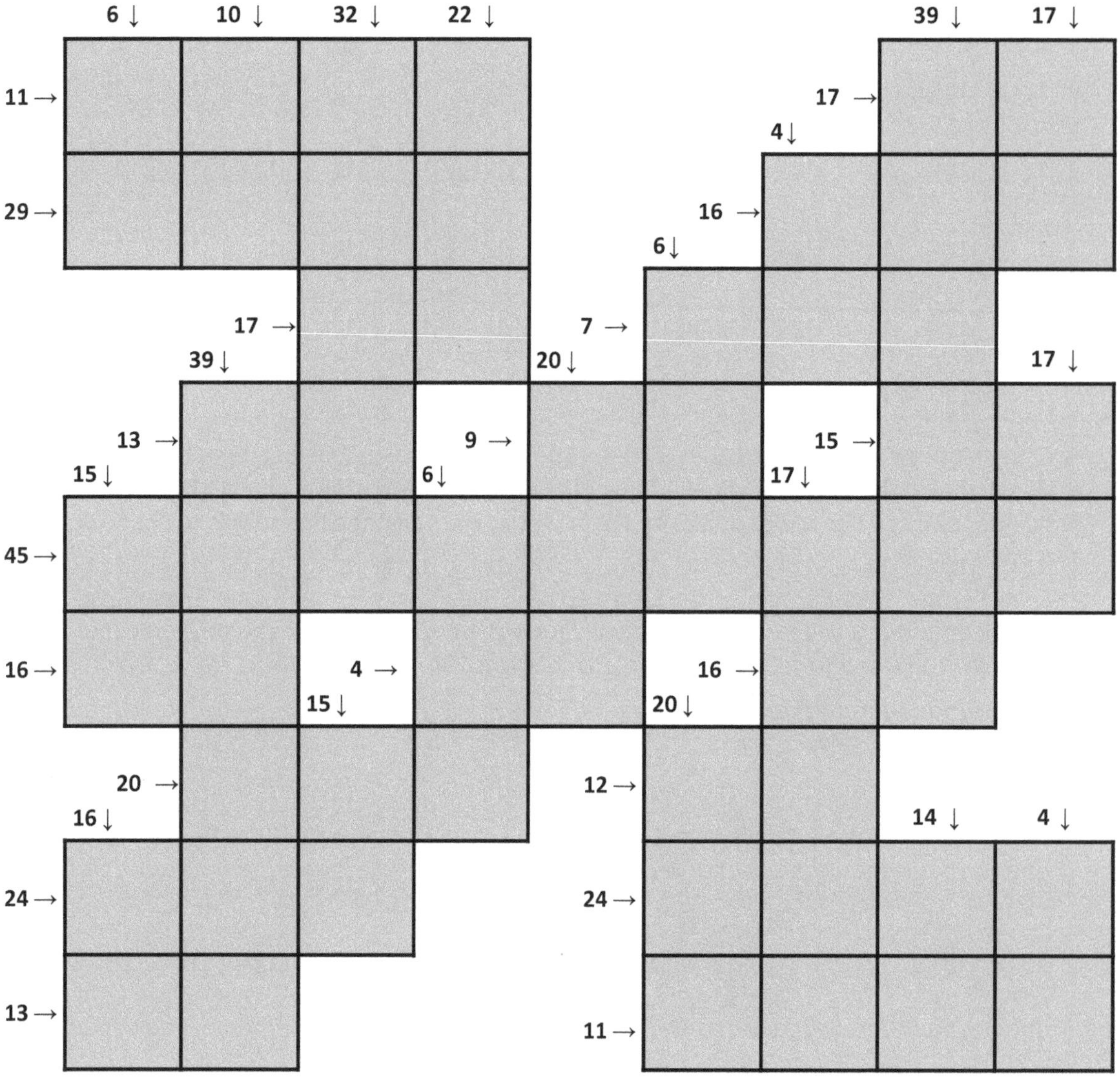
6 ↓
10 ↓
32 ↓
22 ↓
39 ↓
17 ↓
11 →
17 →
4 ↓
29 →
16 →
6 ↓
17 →
7 →
39 ↓
20 ↓
17 ↓
13 →
9 →
15 →
15 ↓
6 ↓
17 ↓
45 →
16 →
4 →
16 →
15 ↓
20 ↓
20 →
12 →
16 ↓
14 ↓
4 ↓
24 →
24 →
13 →
11 →

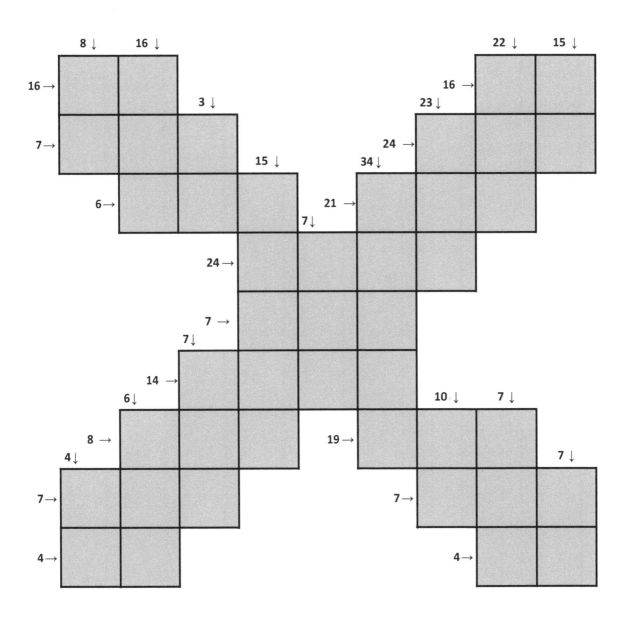

WARM-UP

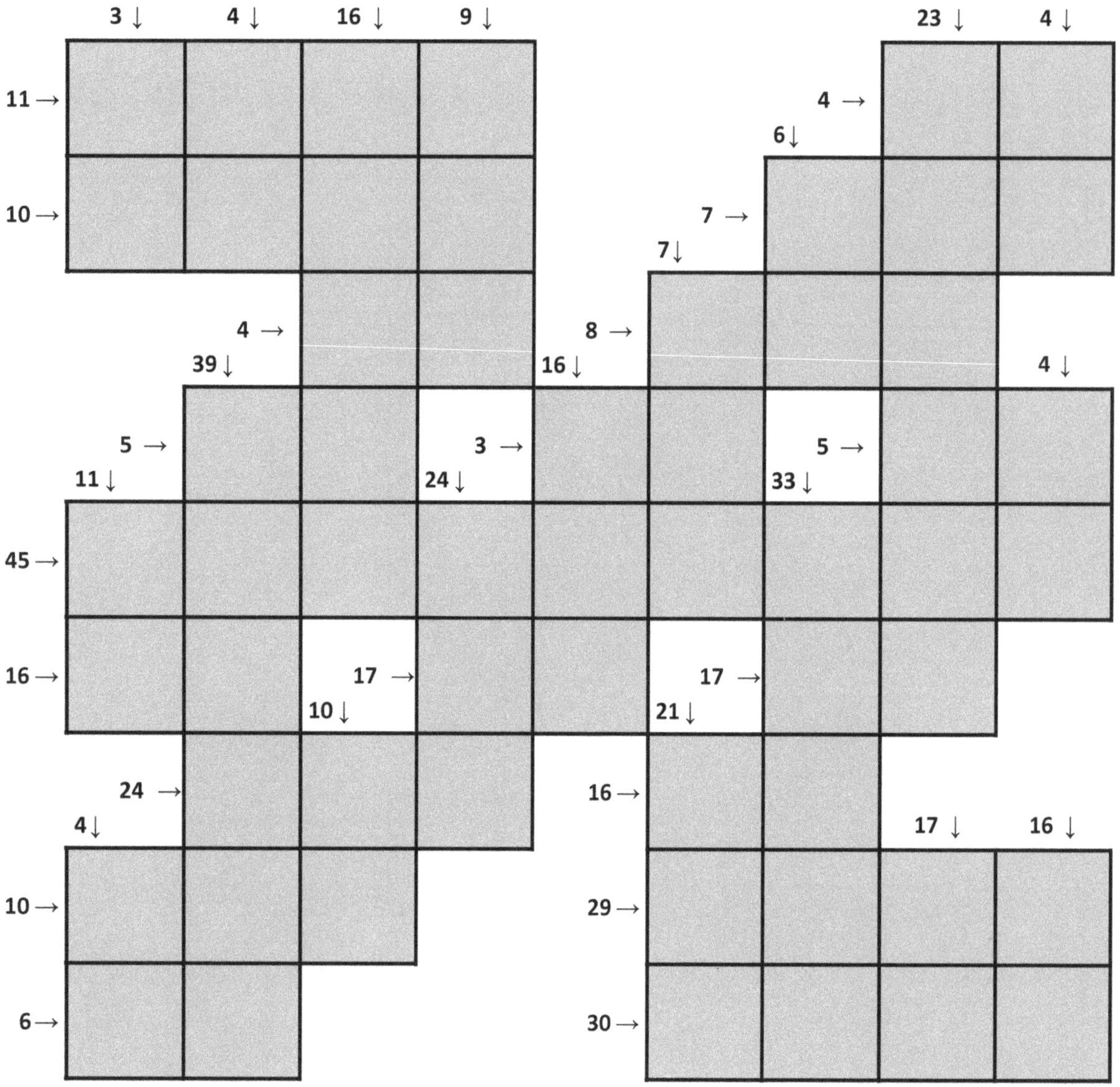

3 ↓
4 ↓
16 ↓
9 ↓
23 ↓
4 ↓
11 →
4 →
6 ↓
10 →
7 →
7 ↓
4 →
8 →
39 ↓
16 ↓
4 ↓
5 →
3 →
5 →
11 ↓
24 ↓
33 ↓
45 →
16 →
17 →
17 →
10 ↓
21 ↓
24 →
16 →
4 ↓
17 ↓
16 ↓
10 →
29 →
6 →
30 →

WARM-UP

TOUGH

9 ↓　7 ↓　　14 ↓　16 ↓

3 →　　　16 →

40 ↓　　　7 ↓　　　40 ↓

41 →

10 ↓　　　　　　　　　9 ↓

14 →　　6 →　　　3 →

　　7 ↓　　　23 ↓

7 →　　　　　23 →

　　　　　16 →

9 →　　　　　　16 ↓

9 ↓

7 →　　　　20 →

　　9 ↓　3 ↓　12 ↓

17 →　7 →　　　17 →

6 ↓　　　17 ↓

29 →

3 →　　16 →

TOUGH

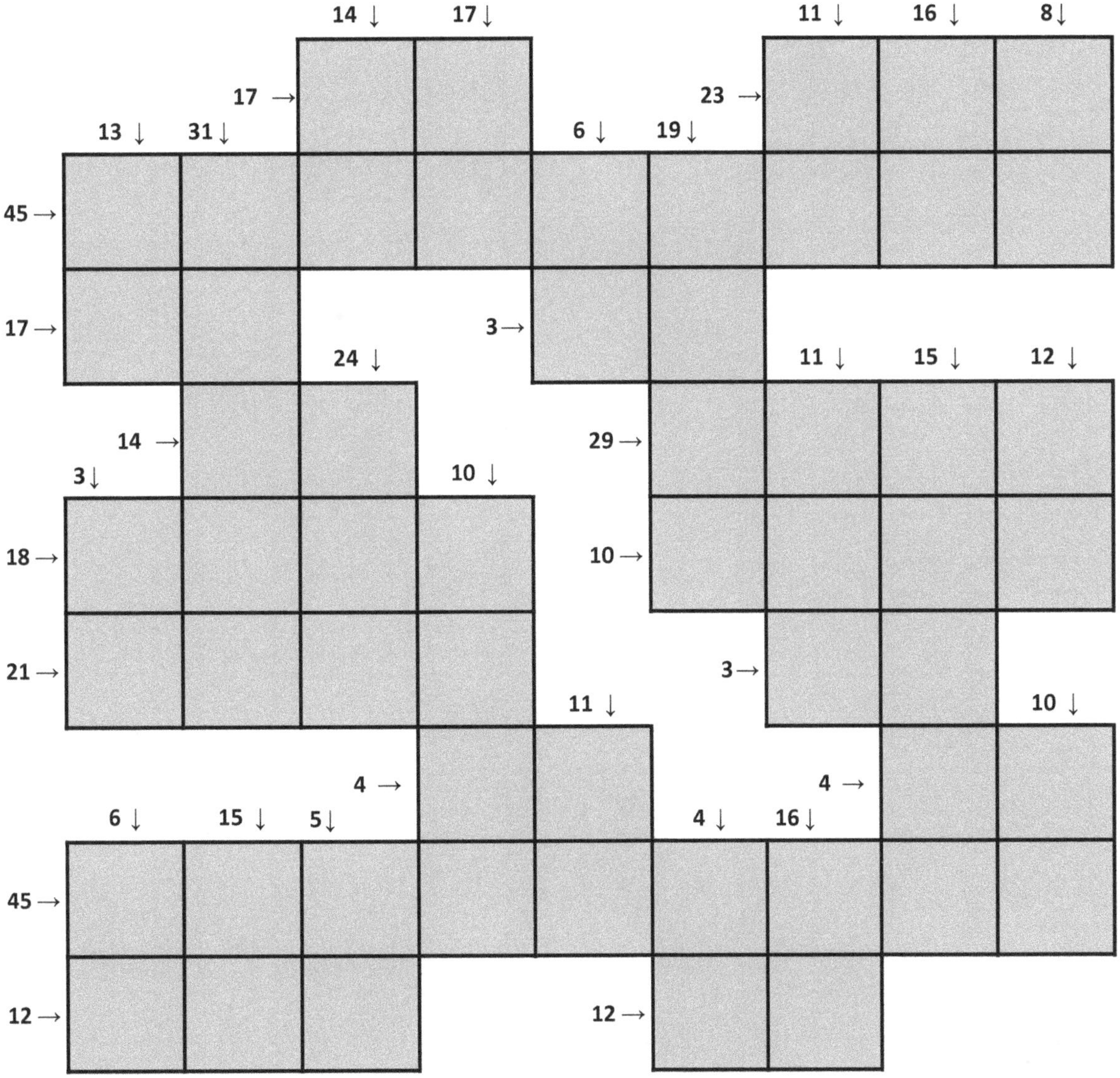
14 ↓
17 ↓
11 ↓
16 ↓
8 ↓
17 →
23 →
13 ↓
31 ↓
6 ↓
19 ↓
45 →
17 →
3 →
24 ↓
11 ↓
15 ↓
12 ↓
14 →
29 →
3 ↓
10 ↓
18 →
10 →
21 →
3 →
11 ↓
10 ↓
4 →
4 →
6 ↓
15 ↓
5 ↓
4 ↓
16 ↓
45 →
12 →
12 →

9 ↓   6↓   18 ↓   16 ↓

3 →   17 →

41↓   11↓   42 ↓

42 →

17 ↓   17 ↓

16 →   7 →   13 →

6↓   6↓

13 →   19 →

6 →   11→

16↓   3 ↓

19 →   10 →

21 ↓   16 ↓   11↓

16 →   24 →   7 →

9↓   5↓

28 →

16 →   3→

TOUGH

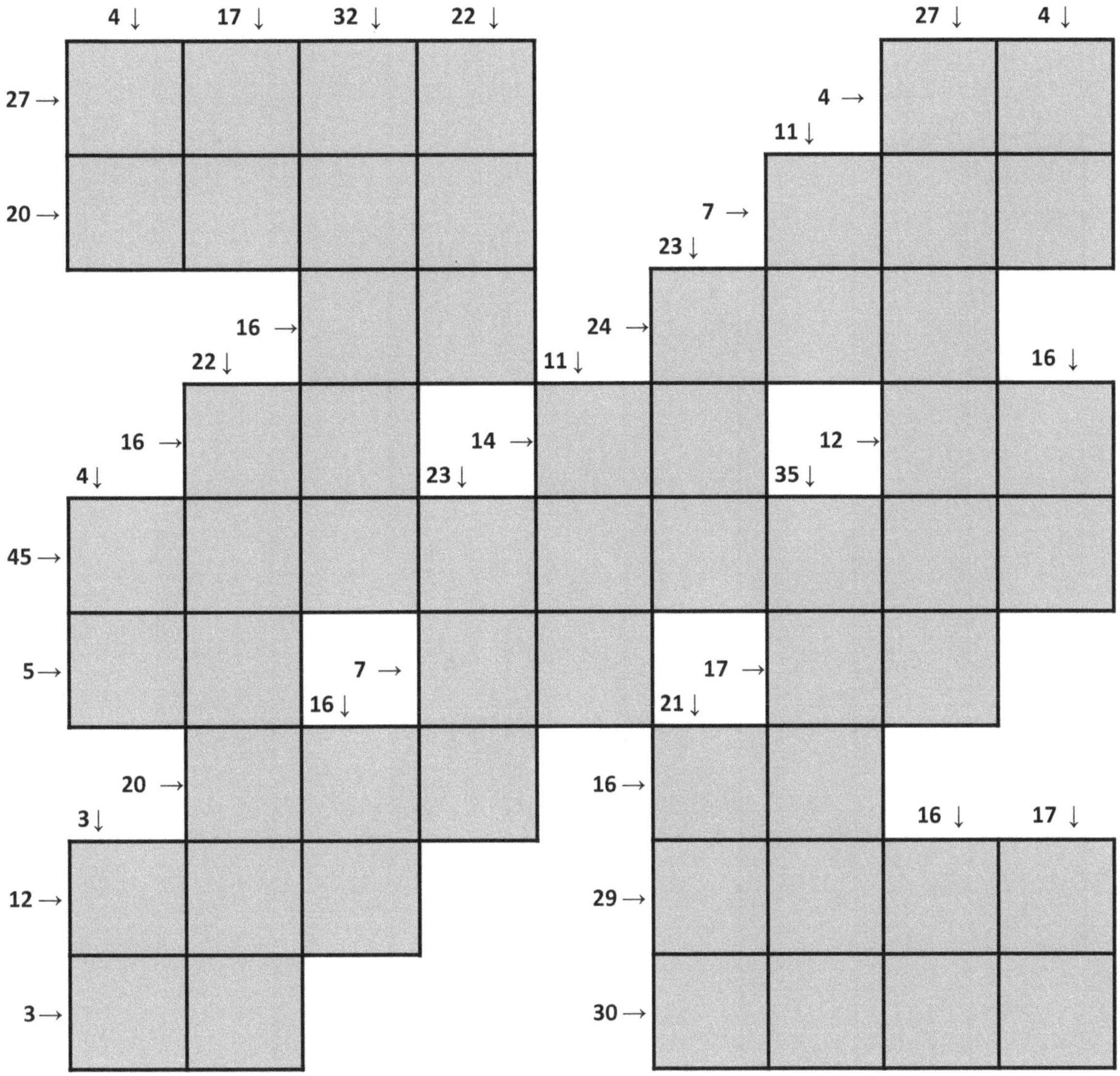
4 ↓
17 ↓
32 ↓
22 ↓
27 ↓
4 ↓
27 →
4 →
11 ↓
20 →
7 →
23 ↓
16 →
24 →
22 ↓
11 ↓
16 ↓
16 →
14 →
12 →
4 ↓
23 ↓
35 ↓
45 →
5 →
7 →
17 →
16 ↓
21 ↓
20 →
16 →
3 ↓
16 ↓
17 ↓
12 →
29 →
3 →
30 →

TOUGH

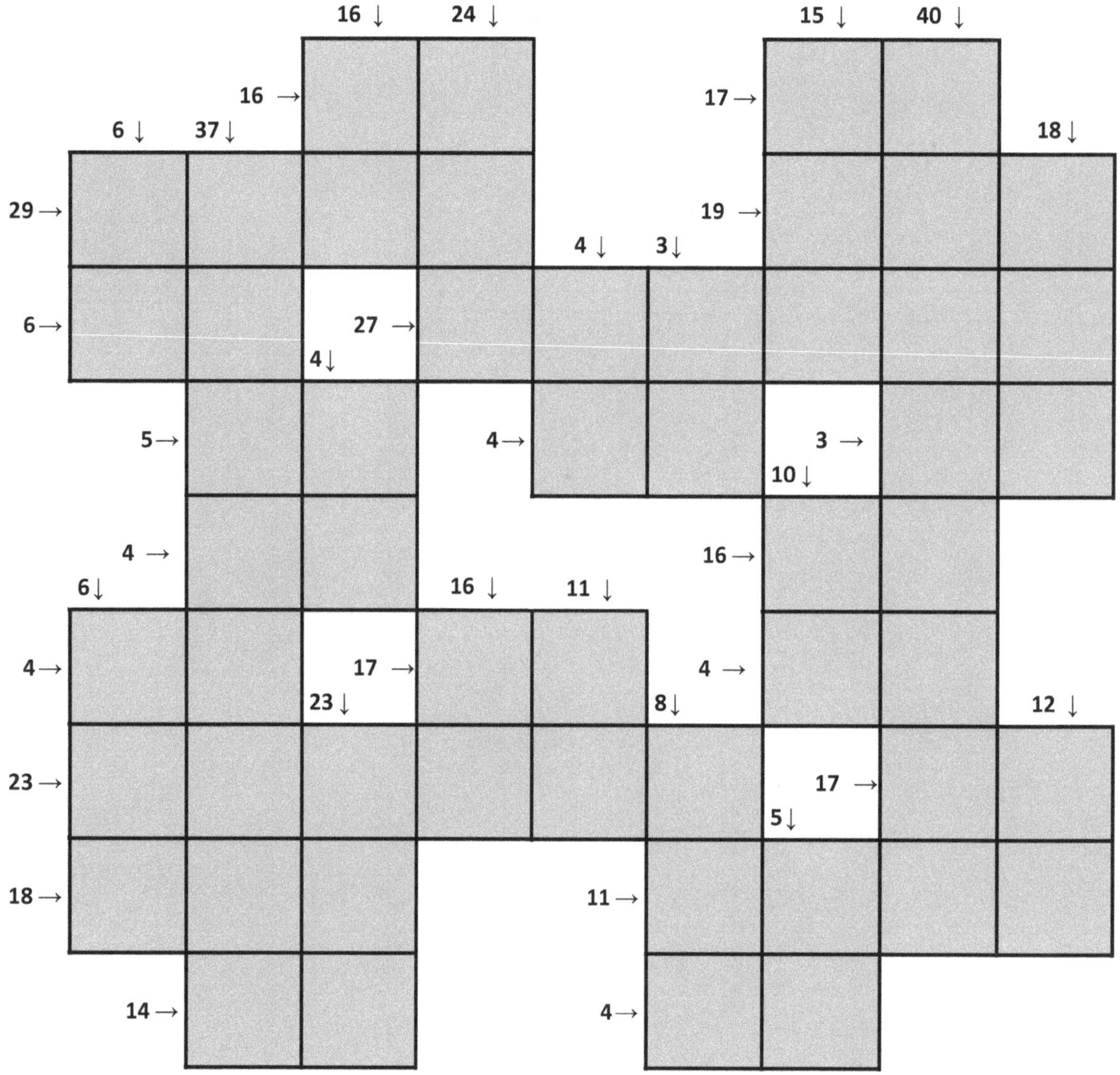

16 ↓
24 ↓
15 ↓
40 ↓
16 →
17 →
6 ↓
37 ↓
18 ↓
29 →
19 →
4 ↓
3 ↓
6 →
27 →
4 ↓
5 →
4 →
3 →
10 ↓
4 →
16 →
6 ↓
16 ↓
11 ↓
4 →
17 →
23 ↓
4 →
8 ↓
12 ↓
23 →
17 →
5 ↓
18 →
11 →
14 →
4 →

TOUGH

Kakuros   **137**

TOUGH

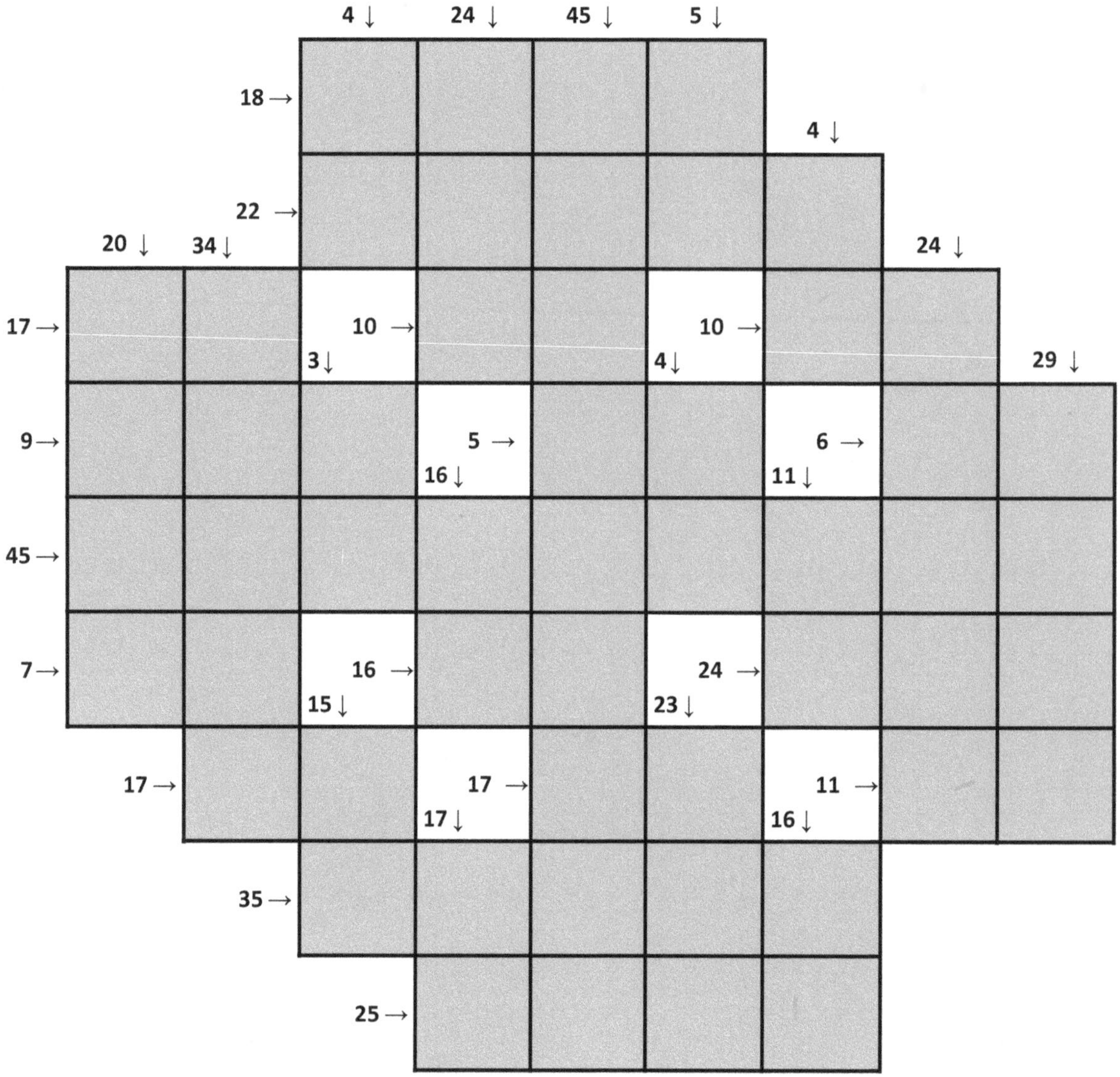
4 ↓
24 ↓
45 ↓
5 ↓
18 →
4 ↓
22 →
20 ↓
34 ↓
24 ↓
17 →
10 →
3 ↓
10 →
4 ↓
29 ↓
9 →
5 →
16 ↓
6 →
11 ↓
45 →
7 →
16 →
15 ↓
24 →
23 ↓
17 →
17 →
17 ↓
11 →
16 ↓
35 →
25 →

HARD-CORE

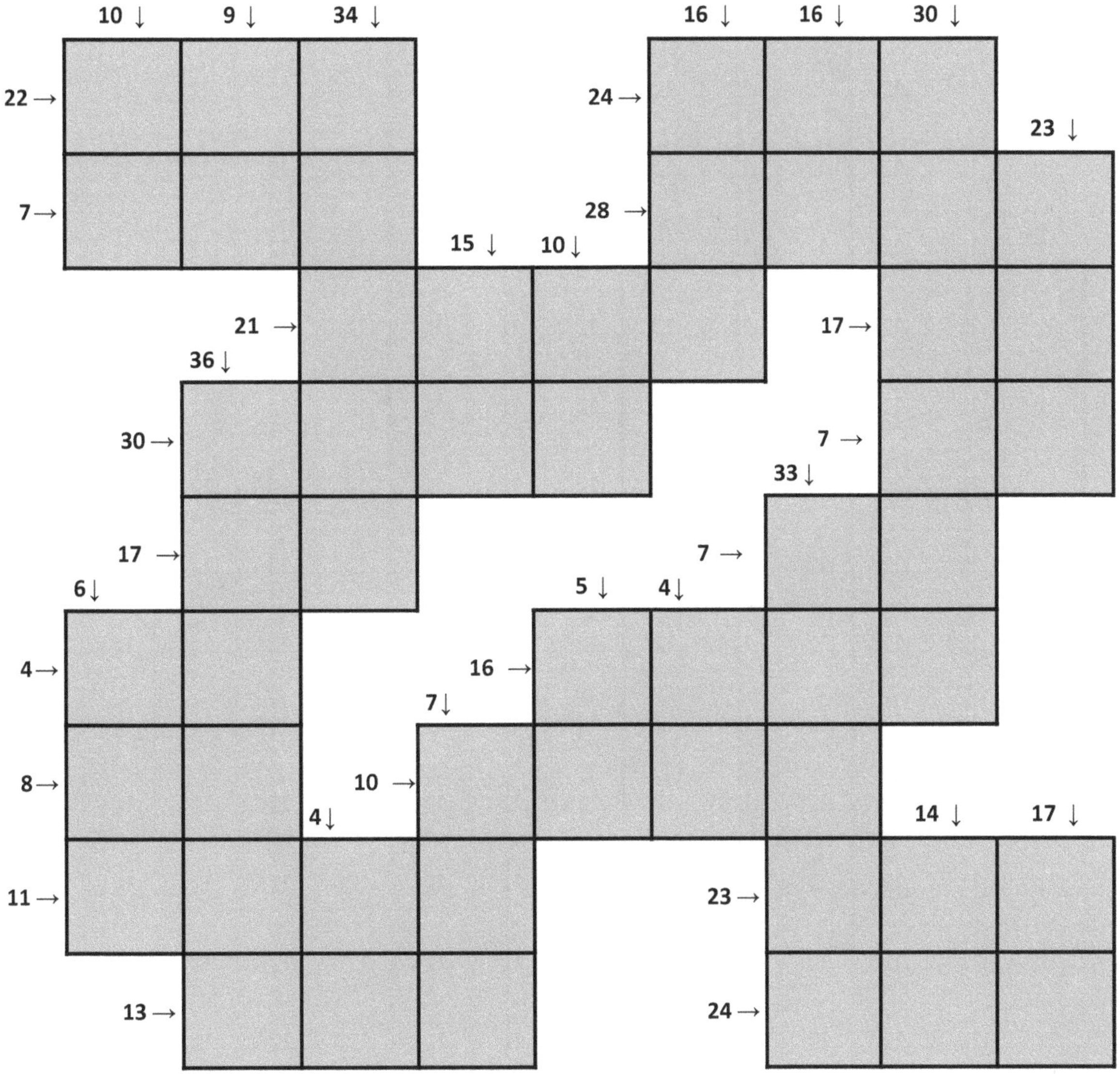
10 ↓
9 ↓
34 ↓
16 ↓
16 ↓
30 ↓
22 →
24 →
23 ↓
7 →
28 →
15 ↓
10 ↓
21 →
17 →
36 ↓
30 →
7 →
33 ↓
17 →
7 →
6 ↓
5 ↓
4 ↓
4 →
16 →
7 ↓
8 →
10 →
4 ↓
14 ↓
17 ↓
11 →
23 →
13 →
24 →

HARD-CORE

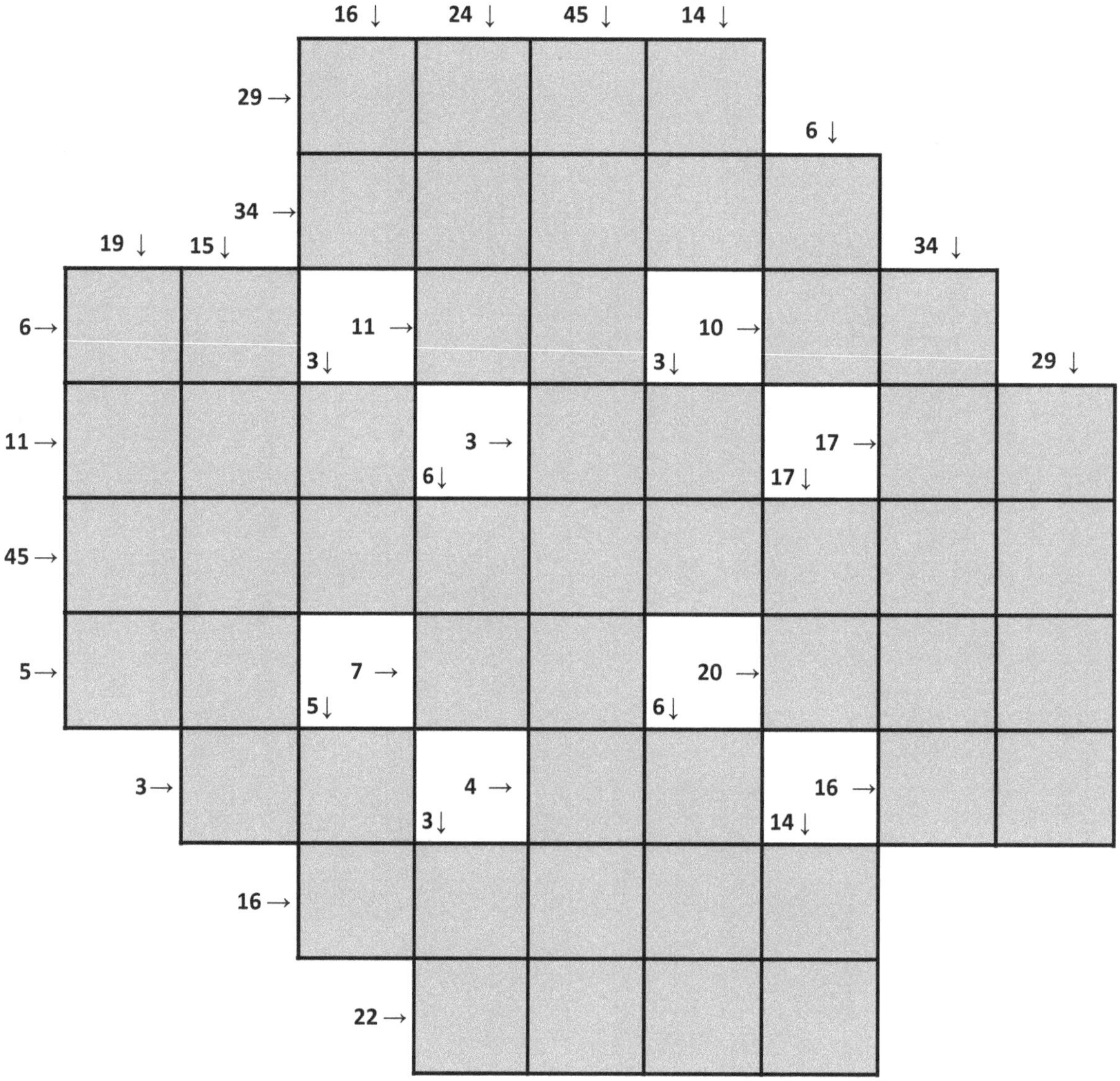

16 ↓
24 ↓
45 ↓
14 ↓
29 →
6 ↓
34 →
19 ↓
15 ↓
34 ↓
6 →
11 →
3 ↓
10 →
3 ↓
29 ↓
11 →
3 →
6 ↓
17 →
17 ↓
45 →
5 →
7 →
5 ↓
20 →
6 ↓
3 →
4 →
3 ↓
16 →
14 ↓
16 →
22 →

HARD-CORE

HARD-CORE

HARD-CORE

HARD-CORE

HARD-CORE

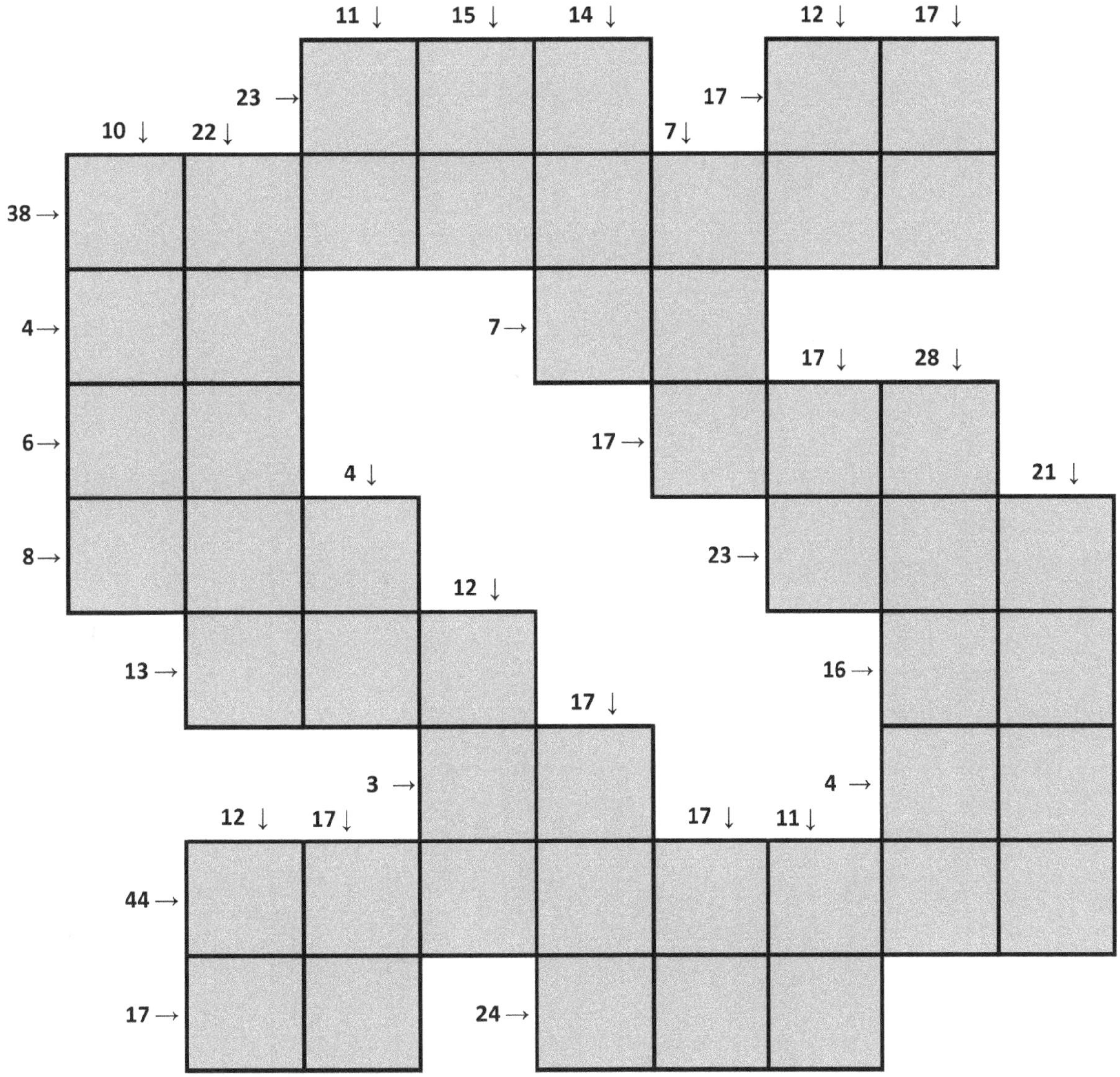
11 ↓
15 ↓
14 ↓
12 ↓
17 ↓
23 →
17 →
10 ↓
22 ↓
7 ↓
38 →
4 →
7 →
17 ↓
28 ↓
6 →
17 →
4 ↓
21 ↓
8 →
23 →
12 ↓
13 →
16 →
17 ↓
3 →
4 →
12 ↓
17 ↓
17 ↓
11 ↓
44 →
17 →
24 →

HARD-CORE

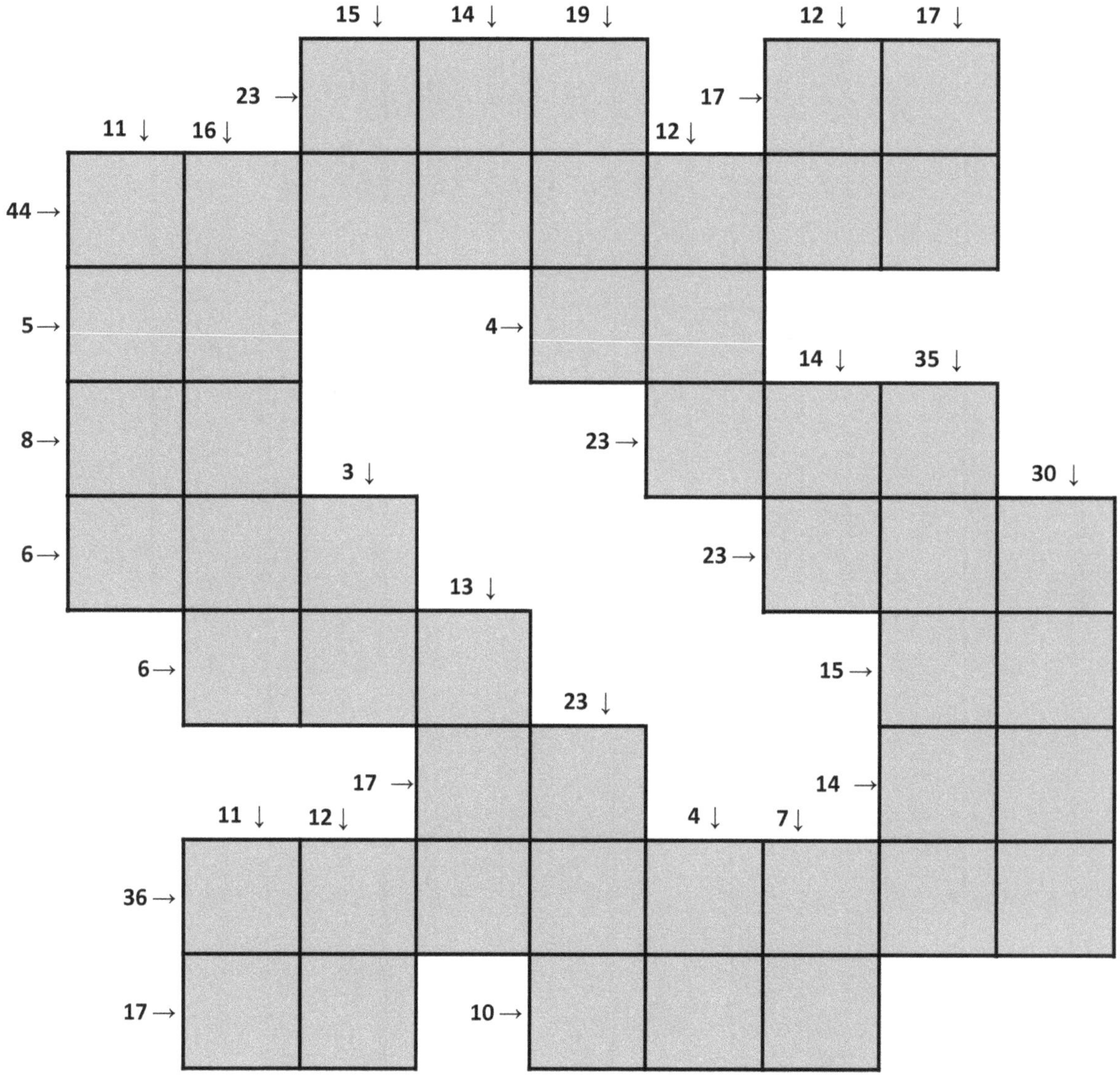
15 ↓
14 ↓
19 ↓
12 ↓
17 ↓
23 →
17 →
11 ↓
16 ↓
12 ↓
44 →
5 →
4 →
14 ↓
35 ↓
8 →
23 →
3 ↓
30 ↓
6 →
23 →
13 ↓
6 →
15 →
23 ↓
17 →
14 →
11 ↓
12 ↓
4 ↓
7 ↓
36 →
17 →
10 →

HARD-CORE

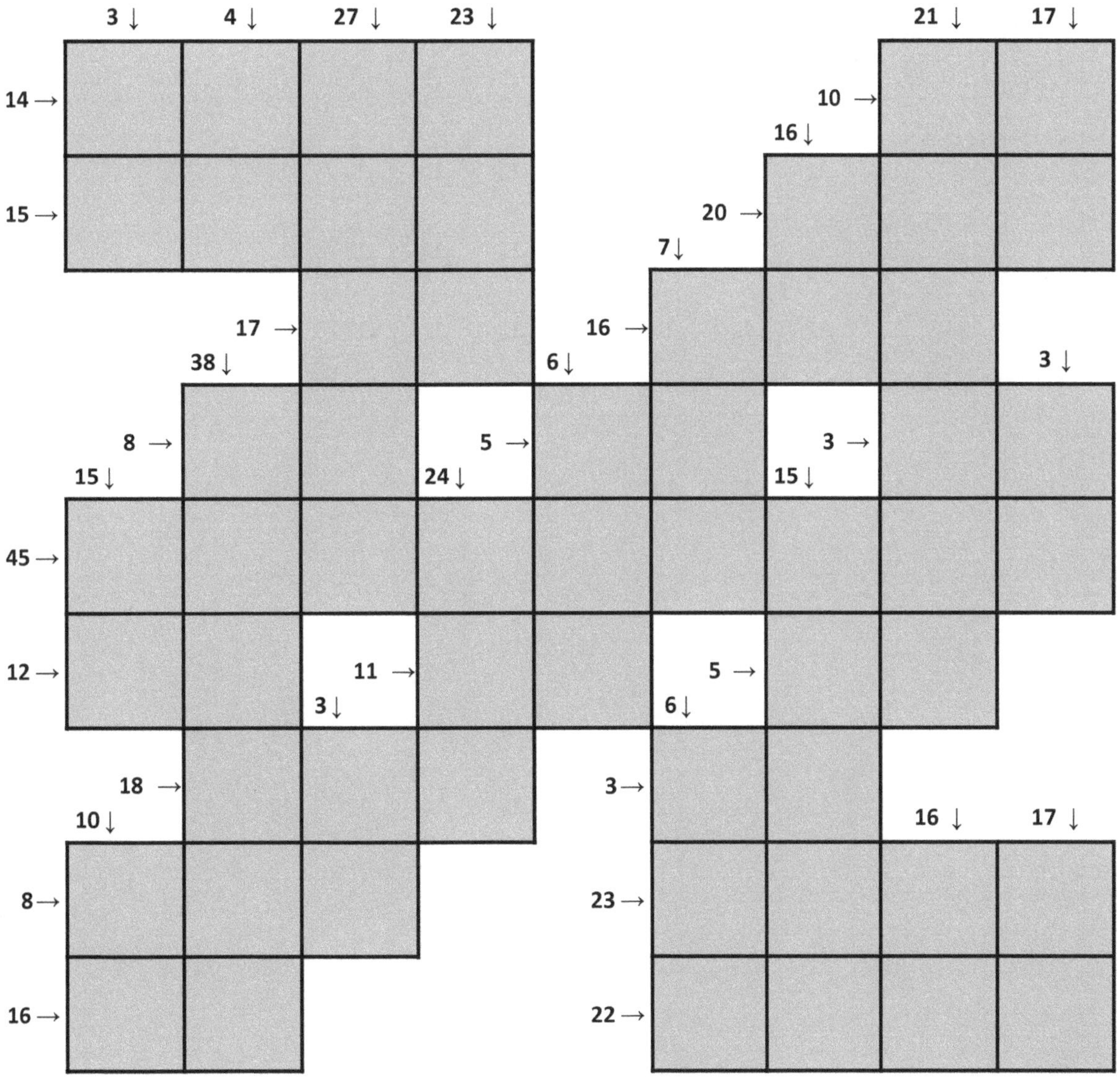
3 ↓
4 ↓
27 ↓
23 ↓
21 ↓
17 ↓
14 →
10 →
16 ↓
15 →
20 →
7 ↓
17 →
16 →
38 ↓
6 ↓
3 ↓
8 →
5 →
3 →
15 ↓
24 ↓
15 ↓
45 →
12 →
11 →
5 →
3 ↓
6 ↓
18 →
3 →
10 ↓
16 ↓
17 ↓
8 →
23 →
16 →
22 →

CRYPTOGRAMS

Cryptograms are a type of puzzle based upon the early days of cryptography, or the science of transmitting messages securely. Before the invention of computers, secret messages were often protected using a *cipher*, or scheme of replacing or rearranging the individual letters in the message.

For example, a simple numerical cipher might replace each letter of the alphabet with a number: A becomes 1, B becomes 2, C becomes 3, and so on. Suppose you have the following sensitive message, or *plaintext*:

THE ENEMY IS COMING!

This would be represented in the following encoded message, or *ciphertext*:

20-8-5   5-14-5-13-25   9-19   3-15-13-9-14-7

Most ciphers fall into one of two broad categories: The example above is a *substitution* cipher, in which each letter (or group of letters) in the plaintext is replaced with a number, symbol, word, or other letter(s) of the alphabet. A *transposition* cipher is one in which the letters are rearranged; for instance, the plaintext above might be reversed to spell:

!GNIMOC SI YMENE EHT

Today, much more advanced mathematical algorithms are used to achieve this type of security, which are impossible to execute by hand. However, codebreaking aficionados still create and solve cipher messages for fun. A *cryptogram* is simply a puzzle where the solver is asked to decode a message.

(Cryptogram clues on page 161.)

LOVE THY NEIGHBOR

Hello, my friend! These first few cryptograms will be substitution ciphers, with logical rules for how the substitutions work. Good luck!

QFNFNAFQ JE ZPV FUFQ MFFC B GFKOJMH GBMC ZPVKK EJMC PMF BS SGF FMC PE ZPVQ BQN

BT ZPV HQPX PKCFQ ZPV XJKK CJTDPUFQ SGBS ZPV GBUF SXP GBMCT PMF EPQ GFKOJMH ZPVQTFKE SGF PSGFQ EPQ GFKOJMH PSGFQT

_____

_____

_____

_____

SECOND SHIFT

Here's another relatively simple cryptogram. Hopefully you won't have to work overtime to solve it!

VJGTG KU PQ VKOG HQT EWV-CPF-FTKGF OQPQVQPA. VJGTG KU VKOG HQT YQTM. CPF VKOG HQT NQXG. VJCV NGCXGU PQ QVJGT VKOG.

_____

_____

_____

_____

PUZZLE NUMBER THREE

DSSOB DQRWKHU FDHVDU VKLIW RI WZHOYH: PCS PCDIWTG HTKTC, PUITG GTBDKXCV VH PCS MH. SDVAJ W LKMAP ZVECO DEVIOAHMB EMJPK W DVKHA, DA ZKMAOJVP YVHEIX KMQP. DMA ZECVO ZMAALVAN, AJVFMKUO PDVA OYMAJANU, WVJZ YMKIAO KVQP PDMA KPVDAN OEMZA AJMHEVCDPAJMAMZ.

_____

_____

_____

_____

THAT'S ODD

I can't make heads or tails of this odd speech. Can you?

TO HEED SIN, TO SWIG MOTORS. PENNIES END INK OF TIBIA—ITCHY! EAT FOAMY ANKLET, IOTA SHELL OF EWE HEISTS EON. DEPICT SHY EARL NIECES' "DAY TOFU" IDIOM. ANNOY IT, CHAIR, NAG! EBB UNTO BEEFY LOTUS: RASHES LEFT.

_____

_____

_____

_____

ELEMENT OF SURPRISE

SIP HALPSCSICA PC BCRSBARFALBSICAHCAFPSI LIHSI BTIBAR SARPTIB
ALB ARFNOCA; H KFSINMGB BCRSBARFALBSICA LIHSI SARPTIB ALB
VARPSIN.

_____

_____

_____

_____

UNSCRAMBLE

MOUUY ILSTV EHINT EEPRS ,ELNT ACHNU ORSUY EFLNO EERVY ,AEVW DFINY
EORTU EINRT AEINY CHMMO .EFNT LOOSS ADNOT EHINT AILRS DFNOO OPPRT
IINTU ADENS KLOOT ADORW AHNOT AELNR .DEHT EINRS EHOOT ADLNR ;EHRT
EINOS EHORT BEFIL HITTU .S

_____

_____

_____

_____

UNSCRAMBLE, GROWN-UP

FIOUWY EEORST AHOTTY EGNORW -:IPSU AABESW AFITUU EHLOSU ADEFMO
BORRSY ,CIIKW AEGHRT IIMNSU EHINTW ADNOSW DDENOV EHNOST ,FOORT
EHOUWY BDLNOT ABEELT AEGNOT ADEIOY AFHHTT AEOSTU .ALLOY DLOUUW
AEHOTV AOSTTY ":EHIM AAHOSW AEHSTU $COSTT ,00002 ".EHNT EHOTWY
CDELUX ":AILM ,AHHOW AEPRTT HOSTUY AEHITT !"EHST AEILRY AEHKTT
.EMNOU HNOSTT ADILOT AGINST .CEHMT DEHILR HLNOSU AADLWY GHOSSW
AEFORT AABERR CENOTW ADGORR -NPPUW .EELOP

_____

_____

_____

_____

_____

_____

_____

TV CHANNELS

It's prime time, and I'm just being a couch potato . . . or is there a hidden message behind my channel-surfing?

19 47 37 37 97 83 47 47 7 67 2 53 37 2 5 11 83 19 11 61 11 71 19 11 97 37 37
53 2 97 97 47 73 2 71 19 47 73 67 2 43 7 7 47 37 37 2 61 67 13 47 61 2 31 23 67
67, 2 43 7 13 23 13 71 97 5 11 43 71 67 13 47 61 97 47 73 61 67 47 73 37.

_____

_____

_____

WAR OF THE WORDS

NIFIMAANGNDIIKELFAANGCHO CHORAYHARCHOIMAIMACHOOVEHARCHO
IMANDICHOIER OVESCAANG NDIOVE HISNDIOVEOVENDIOVEOLF
CHOICTCHOOMEANK RAVLFAANGANGIMACHO, RAVNIFANG NDIOVE
ELTCHOOXTCHOLFAANGNDIOVEOLF ANGOTECHO CHOOVECHOIKEANK
HISNDIANGOTESCANIFANG CHOICTCHOOME OXTNDIOLFOTEANGNDIOVEOLF.

ARROWS

INTHP SATGT HEEG. ↓GROM DIOFS AEOES E,ATO UDORI HGDRU AHINH TNRRE
NEOHI DEPPA GCNRP RAHIY REIGG TIEOE NTFII ,YOOL ORURE USUEH ONYUE INTFN
SRNNH E'NUH DSYON TOCUP TOPUS B,OOT OEOOC MDWTO I'GIT NVRGT DIODG
HUAPO JCLOO RBRPA DUUYT DYOHE DUSH. OEAHL OSUES GHEOE UAIYR UUGLH
IL,OA AONER EOOT↓ ↑LEAL WN'RR IAVFP STKEY OTAET NFWHN DUKY' ,YME

THIS WEEK'S STOCK MARKET

[THURS]	MSV +.01	CPVV -.02	MGK +.02	TVIW -.04	OLAK +.04
[TUES]	WYXO -.10	RMA +.07	FZIB -.01	TCLR +.02	MIZ -.08
[MON]	FAA +.14	WKX -.10	XOD +.01	DEA +.11	BPM +.03 DMC+.01
[WED]	SJIY -.05	PCVZ -.01	ZN -.06	PU -.07	BNOC +.05 BVAL+.03
[FRI]	MIBQ +.03	YV -.17	VAL +.03	EKC +.09	QSM -.08

_____

_____

_____

_____

_____

NUMSKULL'S NUMSCRAMBLE

001135 111335 011349 001129 001125 000128 011556 011256 011113 002358
001245 012589 001247 001455 001799 111459 001235 001489 001357 111236
000255 012256 111255 111568 001569 011259 011244 001558 001299 001123
000258 001459 001457 001229 012556 011335 011256 000256 111255 19

_____

_____

_____

_____

_____

NUMSKULL'S NEW NUMSCRAMBLE

000258 001158 111459 001122 001135 001144 001126 001899 011359 001226
001258 012355 011248 000258 111248 001159 011145 001225 011455 011568
011999 001299 011248 012459 001257 000114 001226 002358 111258 001245
001389 011259 000268 001558 011568 001125 111268 011578 011599 001456
001445 111459 000258 111248 001159 011145 001225 011134

NOTABLY NASTIER NUMSCRAMBLE

00114459 00012225 00022559 00111449 00001256 00112689 00115599
00112445 00012258 01112569 00113445 01223558 00112259 00005566
00111489 00012578 01112568 00011589 00014578 00112245 00122455
01113558 01123568 00001258 00122258 00012558 01112288 00115569
00112258 00002899 00111248 00112558 00113455 00015568 00112245
11122235 00002455 01222345 01115589

THE JOY OF MUSIC

_____

_____

_____

YOU'RE ON YOUR OWN

In the previous puzzles, all of the cipher mechanisms could be deduced through logical mappings, with some help from the puzzle titles and descriptions. Time to take off the training wheels! The following cryptograms don't necessarily follow any neat rules like "shift each letter of the alphabet over by one." Rather, you'll need to think like a real codebreaker. You may use a combination of trial and error and _letter frequency analysis_: symbols that appear more frequently in the ciphertext are likely to be Es, Ts, and As.

H DEEV GC MEE QT CID NEPLGT PDV GC OCDGHDLE GC NE ZEQHDVEV GSPG
H PQ EDCLFS, GSPG H PQ ICZGST CX WCJE IHGSCLG EXXCZG, GSPG H PQ
NEPLGHXLW, GSPG GSE GEYGLZE CX QT SPHZ PDV GSPG GSE MSPAE CX
QT OLZJEM, GSE MHKE CX QT WHAM, GSE OCWCZ CX QT MBHD, PDV GSE
XEEWHDFM GSPG H SPJE PZE PWW ICZGST PDV CBPT.

_____

_____

_____

_____

YOU'RE STILL ON YOUR OWN

AJSQRERH DWMHGR OWM PRDNPR MCWI, QJRHR NG SKASOG GWURWIR QW
QRKK OWM QJSQ OWM SHR AHWIL. QJRHR SHR SKASOG PNBBNDMKQNRG
SHNGNIL AJNDJ QRUCQ OWM QW TRKNRER QJSQ OWMH DHNQNDG SHR HNLJQ.
QW USC WMQ S DWMHGR WB SDQNWI SIP BWKKWA NQ QW SI RIP HRVMNHRG
DWMHSLR.

_____

_____

_____

_____

TOUGH TIMES

XJ DFD YFL RNO ORKE. FQTHRNPH HV YFL DMFPCRLVD YMTH XNQTMGQV
LKQVORLML MC HML VFOQJ 30L, HV YFL RNO GORBMDVO, RNO KHFXGMRC,
RNO HVOR. FL HV PRT LMKEVO, MT PRT HFODVO WRO HMX TR YFQE, MT TRRE
HMX QRCPVO TR PVT DOVLLVD MC THV XROCMCP. INT MW HV YFL MC GFMC,
HV CVBVO QVT RC. HV CVBVO LTRGGVD LXMQMCP FCD QFNPHMCP - VBVC
YHMQV LTONPPQMCP TR INTTRC HML LHMOT, VBVC YHMQV NLMCP TYR KFCVL
TR PVT HMXLVQW FKORLL THV ORRX TR PMBV XJ XRX F EMLL. HV UNLT YREV
NG F QMTTQV VFOQMVO FCD YROEVD F QMTTQV HFODVO.

_____

_____

_____

_____

_____

_____

DON'T WAIT FOR A SIGN

@76 7?3&74?4++ =<%4+ 7+ +#4!3<$ =<%4+ #46!4#*3@? ~<$7<8$4
87* 3* !<? <$+@ =<%4 7+ $@?4$^ *>3+ $@?4$3?4++ 3+
5399464?* 96@= 843?1 <$@?4 ^@7 !<? 84 $@?4$^ 4~4?
+766@7?545 8^ #4@#$4 *>4 944$3?1 3= *<$%3?1 <8@7* +*4=+
96@= *>4 +4?+4 *><* /4 !<? ?4~46 97$$^ +><64 *>4 *67*> @9
/>@ /4 <64 3 42#4634?!45 *>3+ <!7*4$^ <* <? 4<6$^ <14

NOBODY WILL HELP YOU

.TTXRRST UCJO DDJG SZM XAXLG T'EVLE AXIBXBXA XTSVRXI .CVR SZM DDV
XQVB .TXQVETJB XQVB UCV UVXLV ZK ZT ,EJ BZAO CAVXD CVR SZM AZ XASDJVO
MI UXKVASZRTJU XI CVR SZM .DDV EV E'CTJ EJ ESI .TTXRRST OZ MBXCX XLE TV
XASDJVO OZ KCJQCJLE XAV SZM .XASDJVO OZ XEVA ASZM XDISZU :MDDVXA
,XDPBJT XEJSW T'EJ ?TTXRRST AZO VDSBAZO V SZM XHJK ZE XB XQJD SZM
UDSZG

NO TWO WAYS ABOUT IT

UUFDPDFDPKPL UOFDUFFIPKUPUF FPFOUFFDPKPL FDPD POFKPIFKPUUK FP
FLPIFKFPPO FPFOUFFDPKPL UOFDUFFIPKUPUF UUFDPDFDPKPL PFUPPDUF
PRFPPDPDFKPD UFFIFK UFFDPOFK. UUFDPDFDPKPL UOFDUFFI FPFOUFFDPKPL
FOFPPL FOFIFPPLFSFK UFFIFK UOPKPIPUFL.

THE MOTHER OF ALL CRYPTOGRAMS

CU YJG ZNIINLCUO YGDY, GQGBK 5YJ LNBF LCII RG BGQGBHGF, HYWBYCUO
LCYJ "RWRK": LJGU KNV JNIF KNVB KRWR CU KNVB WBAH YJG YHBCZ YCAG,
WUF KNV YJCUP ZN WII YJG YJCUOH KNV UWX HWK WUF FN YN GXUGVIZUC
JCA, CY'H W YBGAGUFNVH KYCICRCHUNMHGB. LJWY KNV FN LCYJ ACJ XWU
CUZIVGUXG UNY NUIK ACJ, RVY GQGBKNUG JG AGGYH FUW UNY ZNB W FWK
BN W ANUYJ NB W BWGK RVY ZNB YCAG WUF KYCUBGYG.

CRYPTOGRAM CLUES

Love Thy Neighbor
B (ciphertext) = A (plaintext)

Second Shift
C (ciphertext) = A (plaintext)

Puzzle Number Three
Try a Caesar shift of 3.

That's Odd
The first and second letters of the answer
are T and H, respectively.

Element of Surprise
H (ciphertext) = A (plaintext)

Unscramble
The first word of the answer is "you."

Unscramble, Grown-Up
The last word of the answer is "people."

TV Channels
5 (ciphertext) = C (plaintext)

War of the Words
The first letter of the answer is U.

Arrows
The first letter of the answer is O.

This Week's Stock Market
The first word of the answer is "too."

Numskull's Numscramble
08=H

Numskull's New Numscramble
The last letter is N.

Notably Nastier NumScramble
The first letter is I.

The Joy of Music
𝄐 = R

You're On Your Own
Q (ciphertext) = Y (plaintext)

You're Still On Your Own
J (ciphertext) = H (plaintext)

Tough Times
X (ciphertext) = M (plaintext)

Don't Wait for a Sign
? = N

Nobody Will Help You
M (ciphertext) = Y (plaintext)

No Two Ways About It
The first letter is V.

The Mother of All Cryptograms
C (ciphertext) = I (plaintext)

Page 2

Page 4

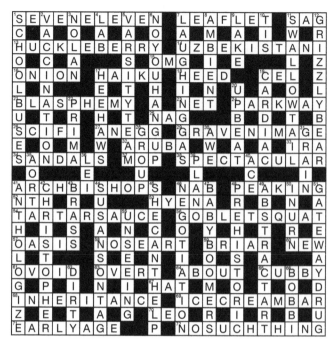

Page 6

Page 8

Page 10

Page 11

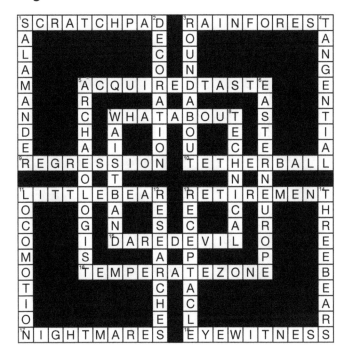

Page 12

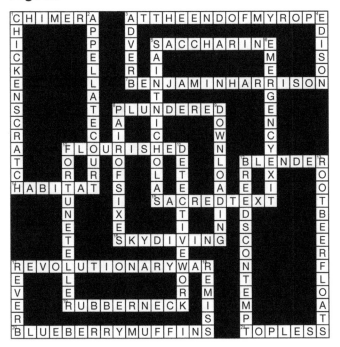

Page 13

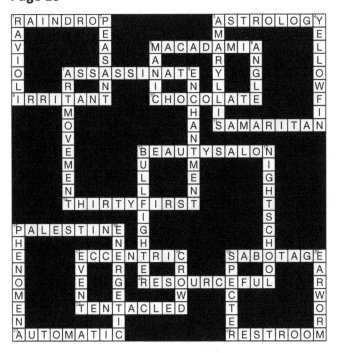

Page 14

```
C O N T R O L G R O U P [ ] T A K E K I N D L Y T O
H . . . . . O . . . . O . . R . . . . . . . . . . R
A . B A C K S E A T . O . I . C A R D I G A N . N .
N . L . . . . . . . O . B . H . . . . . . . E . I .
G . A . . P A R A C H U T I N G . . . . . . . . T .
E . S . . . H . T . L . T . P . R . . . . . . . H .
P . T . I F Y O U R E H A P P Y A N D . E . . O . O .
L . O . . . L . S . . R . . R . . E . D . . E . R . P
A . F . . L . I . E . . . . A . . . D O U B L O O N . T
C . F L O U N C E D . . . . N . . . I . . . A . . . E .
E . . . . . S . A . . . S P O R T S W R I T E R . . R
. S L E E P T A L K I N G . . . . . T . . . A . . . . .
. . . R . . H . . . . . . . . . . . E . . . D . . . A .
. . . A . . . . . . . . . I M B A C K E M I N E M . . .
B R E A K T H E M O L D . . N . . . R . . Y . R . A . .
A . . . I . . R . . . . . E . . . F A L L I B L E . G .
C . D E T O N A T E . . N . S . . I . . O . . I . N . N
K . E . . . N . P . . M . . A . . N . . E . . I . . . .
H . V . S P I R I T U A L L E A D E R . . . . . S . F .
A . E . . . . O . . . S . . L . . S . . E . . . T . I .
N . L . T H E R M O M E T E R . . . E . . O . . . . C .
N . O . . . . N . . . N . . . . . . R . . O . . . . E .
. . . P A V E M E N T . . . . N . . . N . . Y O D E L L E D
. . . . . . . . . . . . T . . . . . E . . T . . . . . C .
L A S T R E S P E C T S . . . S E A R C H E N G I N E
```

Page 15

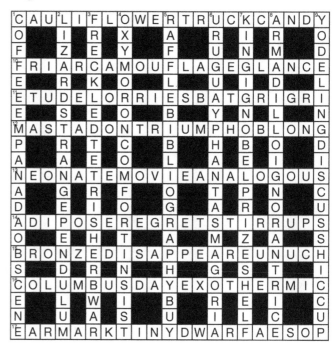

```
C A U L I F L O W E R T R U C K C A N D Y
O . . I . R . X . A . R . I . R . . . O .
F . . Z . E . Y . F . U . N . M . . . D .
F R I A R C A M O U F L A G E G L A N C E
E . . R . K . O . L . U . I . D . . . L .
E T U D E L O R R I E S B A T G R I G R I N
E . . S . E . O . B . Y . N . L . . . N .
M A S T A D O N T R I U M P H O B L O N G
P . . R . T . C . B . H . B . O . . . D .
A . . A . E . O . L . A . E . I . . . I .
N E O N A T E M O V I E A N A L O G O U S
A . . G . R . F . O . T . P . N . . . C .
D . . E . I . O . G . A . R . O . . . U .
A D I P O S E R E G R E T S T I R R U P S
O . . E . H . T . A . M . Z . A . . . S .
B R O N Z E D I S A P P E A R E U N U C H
S . . D . R . N . H . G . S . T . . . I .
C O L U M B U S D A Y E X O T H E R M I C
E . . L . W . I . B . R . E . I . . . C .
N . . U . A . S . U . I . L . C . . . U .
E A R M A R K T I N Y D W A R F A E S O P
```

Page 16

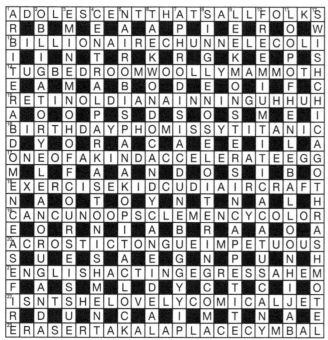

```
A D O L E S C E N T T H A T S A L L F O L K S
R . B . M . E . A . A . P . I . E . R . O . W
B I L L I O N A I R E C H U N N E L E C O L I
I . I . N . T . R . K . R . G . K . E . P . S
T U G B E D R O O M W O O L L Y M A M M O T H
E . A . M . A . B . O . D . E . O . I . F . C
R E T I N O L D I A N A I N N I N G U H H U H
A . O . O . P . S . D . S . O . S . M . E . I
B I R T H D A Y P H O M I S S Y T I T A N I C
D . Y . O . R . A . C . A . E . E . I . L . A
O N E O F A K I N D A C C E L E R A T E E G G
M . L . F . A . A . N . D . O . S . I . B . O
E X E R C I S E K I D C U D I A I R C R A F T
N . A . O . T . O . Y . N . T . N . A . L . H
C A N C U N O O P S C L E M E N C Y C O L O R
E . O . R . N . I . A . B . R . A . A . O . A
A C R O S T I C T O N G U E I M P E T U O U S
S . U . E . S . A . E . G . N . P . U . N . H
E N G L I S H A C T I N G E G R E S S A H E M
F . A . S . M . L . D . Y . C . T . C . I . O
I S N T S H E L O V E L Y C O M I C A L J E T
R . D . U . N . C . A . I . M . T . N . A . E
E R A S E R T A K A L A P L A C E C Y M B A L
```

Page 18

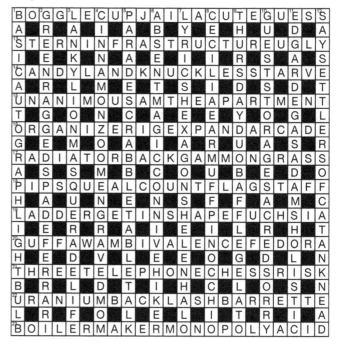

```
B O G G L E C U P J A I L A C U T E G U E S S
A . R . A . I . A . B . Y . E . H . U . D . A
S T E R N I N F R A S T R U C T U R E U G L Y
I . E . K . N . A . E . I . I . R . S . A . S
C A N D Y L A N D K N U C K L E S S T A R V E
A . R . L . M . E . T . S . I . D . S . D . T
U N A N I M O U S A M T H E A P A R T M E N T
T . G . O . N . C . A . E . E . Y . O . G . L
O R G A N I Z E R I G E X P A N D A R C A D E
G . E . M . O . A . I . A . R . U . A . S . R
R A D I A T O R B A C K G A M M O N G R A S S
A . S . S . M . B . C . O . U . B . E . D . O
P I P S Q U E A L C O U N T F L A G S T A F F
H . A . U . N . E . N . S . F . F . A . M . C
L A D D E R G E T I N S H A P E F U C H S I A
I . E . R . R . A . I . E . I . L . R . H . T
G U F F A W A M B I V A L E N C E F E D O R A
H . E . D . V . L . E . E . O . G . D . L . N
T H R E E T E L E P H O N E C H E S S R I S K
B . R . L . D . T . I . H . C . L . O . S . N
U R A N I U M B A C K L A S H B A R R E T T E
L . R . F . O . L . E . L . I . T . R . I . A
B O I L E R M A K E R M O N O P O L Y A C I D
```

Page 20

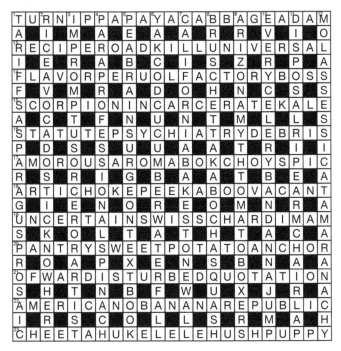

Page 22

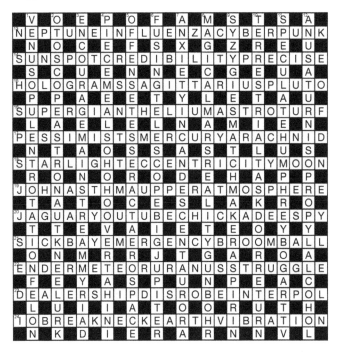

Page 25

Page 26

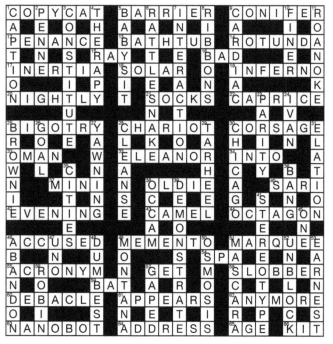

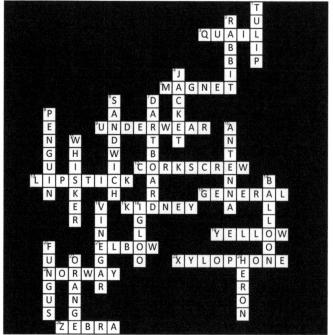

Page 36

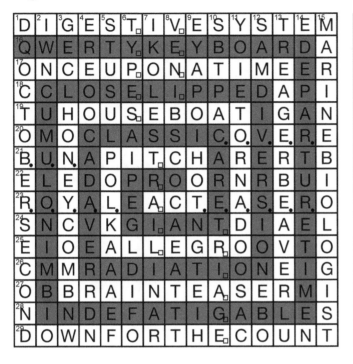

Page 38

Page 40

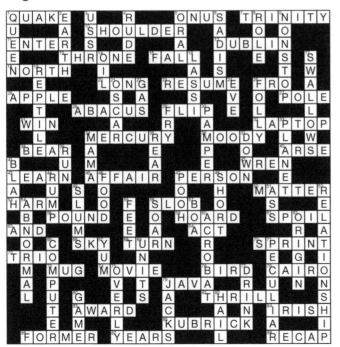

Page 42

Page 46

```
O M P Y I C A K L I A T R E G I T A I E S R B M O
N T A E E A U B A N A N A I O R U M R A I S I N U
R A E S A F L A L L E T A I C C A R T S M I A S A
S R C A U N I H U R S M O R Y S A K U E N A I H C
O N F E E P U K O N M O N U R E R I N K O E N C I
O O B E P A E T C I A O H A T L R P S A O E O K K
T N B E B R M R B R C T K L A C E A N C M T M S A
E A S C O A E S M U T T Y N P S O D C Y E P U O O
A T A P A V T T U A T E U K I T C O U A U A P R E
C I A O T O I B T B N T C C H Y F N A D L E S A N
H L Y I T L C M P U T L E S C F S B M H B E R N H
F O R H L R T M A K B E C R E L A R N T O U O G G
R P R C T B I T T L E E D E T E L R C R T E L E U
E A E A F L M F T E M H E M A S T O O I R A A S O
N E B T L I I E E A U L E M L N E C M B P E T H D
C N W S R E C B S O I I O G O F D K R T T I L E E
H L A I T U M E O N A O A I C E C Y M C S P C R I
V R R P S K S Q E U S R I S O T A R D C U N I B K
A T T S R K A A N E E C R K H N R O W T E I E E O
N C S E C S C R T S L E A O C F A A O G L K I T O
I A E A E O E R M A O P S I T T M D P C C P B S C
L M L W I M A P A C A R T U N L E Z A H K M L E T
L B E M R C L P S B M O B N I C L E A P A U T C B
A E U I K R C R E R I O E E M I K L C A H P L T E
R O I S Y L A D T F O A G O T K R E T C E H I L G
```

Page 47

```
Y D I N L E E L E A D E R S H I P A D A O G S I C
M O I R D L Y R N N O N A I C I T I L O P C U M R
U U Y I N A R N A V F C R Y U L A L I T A V O N E
W O N D E R F U L R E R I U O S S N F N A R R O T
T S Y A S E A O C C E T S R T M A A W P N A E I P
Y U S D O N T I T S E A D R C L E O I E T E G S O
R B T V U U F E T T I O O R L U N R E E N N I C
A T E E R F R T O I R N W A M T M O O L T H A V I
R R E R R M S E N M O T Y I E I N F W I R T D E L
E A M T I E R A I M M T R N T S M E E I E L L L E
N C I I H I R T E I E O E F S E A R M R I N T E H
I T C S Y E O R S O L N S O E B F P C E E P R T S
T I R I A R S T Y Y A F T R R C T I H I R N T T M
I O O N Y F A W O U N I A E E D A R O L C I C C B
S N W G T O R O S E C E U S A Y L N E P H I T E D
D D A O O F L V E G H L R T I O A A E I E I S E Y
T D V T N I E O T R O R A A Y R I N I T N R L A R
E P E O R R A M N S L L N H I V F S R O R S Y F R
L U R T U M R R I S Y F T C T U U M O O U O T L E
R B R R A T B T I I N R O D A S S A B M A R A R B
W I E I A E I R V A S T N A W E T Y N A I R B Y E
I E E O O R E W O L F I L U A C L R N R I I N E U
T H O S P I T A B L E E R S I L H O U E T T E I L
U U N N I Y N Y T I S R E V I N U O E B A E H L B
T S R D L H S E E U C I T S S R E T C A R A H C A
```

Page 48

```
I A A T I F E L D D E P E S A E R C E I I L D G D
D D G D E P W E D D I N G O O I E D R A I N R L H
F K R I N E E L D D E M T B L R E T T A B S E A E
O E E D E T W R O L T P K U O U M S L M W S P T O
U R A I I I R T R L T O M M Y E E A R E Y G P E I
N P S E S M E N W P R E T A E H C E E C E E I M H
T P E I R E R E I E L P M I S N G T A C K S H E Y
A N T T R E I E P L N O F O I N O C K L N O S R H
I I C H E T G I S I M T E T I P S E R I O O Y I T
N A Y G T E E N A E E E T F E H I E E D M M M E U
E T E I A I M R I A R L R E T S I M W E E N M L O
T N K L E E B R S L S V D K D E S P I T E E O P S
H U N F H E O I E P R L E D G N I D D E B K M M E
G O O I T O S M N V O H E T A E E I M N A C M I L
I M D E K T P A B O R L C S N P T K M C I I P P D
L R K I E N O L S O E H F H I D F I R U N H M G D
S R E R A T A E G I I P Y E P L A G A I D T R C A
I M I L Y D N I K P E M M E C A R V S D C E R L W
W Y I M E S P O P N I C M R M D D A E H M D A O N
B S M P M O O E N E S I U R T E K P I L N L M C T
E U A E C C R T M K T V G E E M E C I T E C F K S
T K L K I R R K A Q E L T H T T K N M F K H E E K
M N E E L C R E K W U O N A A E T L R A Q E A T D
A T E T L T I R N T B T D L N Y T A R R T E E M E
P T T D E V R E S E D M H T A U R I P C H R L M P
```

Page 50

```
G O L I S T E N M E R T N R W T G H F A E K C C E
L S E T O E R E R A L O E H N R R A U N T A M R E
I C S E T A R C R A R O R T S T O R E H R E E A O
A A T N A G E V R T E H O R O I W G Q C K R A T O
R L E Y B H O R A E S E F A H P L G A A M T N E G
G D R T G L E P R E B P R E P T S S O T R S E R B
T H E R B R R C L P R M R H T R L H C T E D E H L
C Q G A R T T P Q A G S E I Y E N O M A V E S P I
U E G E O S E E L R I D C V N R E D C C O E C A N
S G A H O O T T E G A G R T O G P J S A R R H R D
N Q J P M P L E V H A S O S W O E A A A E G G E G D
V J U A A M R F O V S R W T L S H G G O O E A N E
S N D I G O B F R E R T N L C E R G E T O B P E B
A T N O R C O U G T G P E R A A O E V C V R L E M
L C W T H E S B J O M N O V R T I D W Y C O O R E
S A O E S O P M O C R W E E E T J T T R H O R G A
C R R K D E T S I L D N R T F A A E J M E K T S G
A T G N E N E A B A A S I G F C E N R N A E A L S
L E N I S S I E E G G T E D U K N O G E T R P A U
E R D L E P H A M A E R T S B S E M T N T R O C R
D O E B R G O P R S A I U N N P A G P E O R P P E
E B V B E G A L T G E U S T O R K P E E N R A O E
E A A E O R R R L O R Q G E O I V N G A E R A C O
R H E E T P A E P E S S O A N N I E Y C S H R F E
E T H Y P P H M A H R O N D B T E E S E R C S P P
```

Page 52

```
T P N N E E E P T Y N E R P Y Y D I O R S Y G O E
E E I K L E N P C R P A N H S W I N W L B E U R V
P E V E O P C L P T N T E A S L L E O L C R T H Y
R T U I K O O G R L A G E E R Y D A C S S C Y S T
E T C E L R U M E M R V E V U Y L L L A N J A P O
C A C E Y T T L T A D I C R U R Y L O N P O C U Z
R L C O Y N W I R O A Y H H T U N G K G A W L R R
E E L J T A O S H Y W A S Y S K I I N B E D I L I
R A E H R E Z A E T Y Y R S Y E W C N A R I L Y E
P K V T S P M E T R V T K A G R V I T I E V N R W
T V R R T C E Y P P I T E C O R Y T L G E L S J U
T E A R U I P T O N C V R B O O I A D E N T T O I
R I P E I P A R O P E V A I R T R Y N G R R G O R
D R E W M I O N G G R A O B D H W W R R N T R I R
P R R F E E E Y N A E L Y Y A U R Y S T P R P C E
I P R T C T Y A E S Z Z P M I T C E L A C I H T T
V T W I S T E R T G U E I U J L O A C L A R E I H
U E T L A N O G U J I E N G C D W R A E S T A V Y
G N O T R Y V Y A G E W G S N E T E A A J T S I L
R E U P E L J R T M V E J K Y V T O Y V L T D R Y
I Y N S A L U O E R T E A C V E E I W V G E N Y I
J P N U R E L O E T L W D T O W E F I E G P U A L
B E I I R T F S R L D P T N I P E R E N S E N F R
Y R S N O V A R R I W A P G W I L Y R C R I E T I
R O T V G E R E V I E D R G H E L O W H F R U P Y
```

Page 53

```
P E P N H A S S O R A N I T D N R H L S A A I T O
E R E B I A P R P P P S E N O L S L I S H T W T S
L C D I R B Y I A T E L I G N S R D T I E N E E E
I R B R E D C P I S E M A B E L E K O L I B S C R
E E E O P M O P O S R H T A N Q O R O F T O D P F
N A U T E H C E G E O T R O L A W O C D E B S L F
T N R I T C I F B M O P U E N T Y R E K S S O G L
O T L R K A A F R N E K O N E Y F S O F M A S L E
E O I E O O M O E A N E H P M E O O T R O R S I S
I E S N U T G K S K O K Y W E L O E Z B H A E A F
S N E P P O I F T W O R P E Z Z M R A S V B I M U
E E N T L A P N A P I A P B C N A O A H E E W E L
P R A A L E O R N S P H R M E N P F S L M U E E T
O T L Y S P T T A T A T O V E R O R I A F S U Q A
U E O A L O W I D N D E G L N I O E F D R E I M I
S R L W A T E T H S T S O U D R R P I E I I T C R
I T A C D E P S B E E B F S S E T E L E N P R O P
E K O O M K I C O I E R P C E R I B R E A P O R A
C E E A P A R T S S E L G O R E I A E S F O N E F
R S Y N T E I U S I N A E D D M I Y A S S L D F U
E B O N T L G B H S I V A K E E N S N O S A I E S
T S P O H O R A S R D I L O R B T F O I S F D D B
L E E P E E W T G U S E P P U M I F E T W F O E O
S A I O J F O R I O I S E P S E C S L C U O O O S
H P I B R P I K A O R E P M B I H T O E R I D S S
```

Page 54

```
R K N N U A D G D S N A U T O W O E I N F R A N L S C E T D
H I A M G O M S R M E N A I T K R K L A U Q E C T N L E G N
N L V O S T I T W O A S T U V E D I I T A T N S E T O M T R
F L E T E S Y F E E L S A D U R B R E Y M E I T O P R I T R
S S L A Y S D H C A E L R E T S S T E Y T E D T T C K T S N
B R O O W W E I C S U S A N T T S Q I S O S G U O H O T E K
I E B R E N N A A G T G S S S U D E N T S P D O T W N I N W
T R T F K E Z A D O H L T S D T O T L E T R U K E H N C W C
R U A M D L I W S S O Z R A S N W H S T S O A L E T N T O N
I T I U N A I F S T M P C R E T O E C V E T W S L I O V E S
C A L S T S R I A L Y I I B I H D T O I C Y O T S L S I B S
S S E E S P E C H O L C T T E O : S U E A O E N R C B S E N
I N O Q U A T G N E R S S R T R P E N T R Y D U T S C N G I
N G S H S T E E A T N O C E P T T E A M S S I D E N I E F F
E L E X I O G A T S T R A C A I N R A W S H I S P A E L T O
H G O O N R I R O Y T E U S N O E C R E T A R N A Q M T E G
E E W N I O A N Y I P A L S T E M E N I L S T O D G M A R D
Y D I E U G L T T W A P R C A T O G A L E M O F R U S C T
J U N A G A J S T E A S Y A N M A A S A I E K U E B S A A
A E S E C I T I A I P V C M R T O T T E R D H T T G N A R O
E L D N I N X L D R A A H A I P R E I T F D S E I T I F N N
C T E I D A R L C L H E T O R S T S N T G R E A B T C E D I
T O P T W O S N D S I E C A I O Y N A S U A O O R E R T A E
I T E S A R B C H I N E S E Y B E T O A R A E R I O F O D D
O N N Y N N O S R M C C E K L L S N O C N V E O D R T A E
N E D R A L R A T R V N A F W O I R S E S I E R S S H R E
W N C N R D E B U M D T U E L R F N T I T L S E T V E S S E
S C E A I S I N A T E D D R L E K E H U M A N B T E L O O A
S U T H O S A S S A R N I E S H N E L E L U S A F N T E N A
E U F L I C T T H O J K L M R S E H E A S Y A C N E E A E O
```

Page 55

```
G O A W M L I K C A N O P S S T A I H T C H A U P
S U R O O O N I K C G D Z Z B R S A K E K E G L S
T L F O G L R H L E O G D U B E I P S L P R A H O
C E A S T R G R P E H N I Y H T T B N U M I W L Y
H O M H L M R K H R I R R T K T T E K H E B K H H
C O E H A Z E L P A A A U A A A P R L E O T A S H
H M C E E H A W T Q I S Q W S O O C W S W A H O B
O O C Y E S I Z A I A O C K H O H A H U A B R H H
H I I I W A L Z T P H E L H T O W O U S D W A Q W
E K I P H H E O B Z O Y B M H S I W Q T A I H Y A
H E H P E E H R R H L C R U O O U Q C S C A R B A
E U Z H G C O O R R O P I L M B H S I M S C H L O
K O W K I S H A A H P N L C U A K H A W Z H U E K
O R V Q E N H R H R A F O O B O H A H E O A W U W
O M C H O O Z A S S U U C P A H A B O U C T I R B
A S A O O O P L B I B Q H O N M O O A S E H W E I
O H A A B M S Z B O A U R O Q M U R D A C S H Z P
O H S W H F H Q D M C E E R S M K H L O A I R G O
K O H K H H I A H A K C H N L U W H I C S W A C O
S H O H R H H B M Z Z R L I S E O K T K C H G W H
H K P O C K I I I Z P H S L I E E C O T A I N G H
O M I E E E K T F I R K E E R S E R B O H C R A M
M E T A A H E E N U O W L K C A Z H H O H I O O O
N I D C I O T H E R L O O E S R C T R I O K H H K
K O C E U O H C E C S R G C T C S I B B O N O C R
```

```
R O L I N E E G O O E S I E M E T S S M O M T B B A M
A R H M E E Y M A R L K P U S S A C Y E A O W C A L B
C H W S L A B A N O A N A H M I M I E S D R Y Y N T A
T E E E A E M T E E R E U L E A R U O Y O S R T N U P
I N I I R I O H S W E K I L I L B W N E U F E E N O C
O O B T O P S N E E T I L S N E R O E Y O Y N L T W E
S N O O N O L E H T E R D O G E M H D D U P A C H O M
E L H O E V N T A S I E E O G F A L G A L U U L E H I
A I N T L O U N I I H H O V R O L R I A O C N O B E M
M M D N O M I H D D O W B I U S L E H O L T A V I N E
H E N U O H G H K N H L A V O N L H Y R S N A E R L K
V O A S A T M E N N H M N E B W I M T F O T O T T Y A
I W E T L T A N O U G E T H O I N I H H G I N C E E T
R A N U A T W T O R I T I A H E D W E T I M L A E A E
T I T O W A H N R O O O Y D M M B O A I N M L E I I A
T H A D O T O I V B E W N O L I N A N P G E Y B E L H
R E T D N O T M H A L S N S N A I M O I L M A P C F R
Y A W E M T S T N O E V I P R R A M I V U O N R A Y E
O W L R Y A T O P D I N E A H E E E H I N G O O O E O L
R L U F N L G P B E L V E R T D I M R I L L M N A U E
I D M N C E S L R I M O U C N A C Y H W T Y E I P A I
T E I V L U O M M G Y E Q I T N I F E A R K C A N W N
R A S P I L Y E W H E R G N H E L O E V E R I E A O O
H E E O A N F O N A T I G E R M P W J O E E R W R E K
E H T F M O U T U F E F O E N D F N G L A M E M A T W
H L L I A P M P E R H T E Y O H A I I N E S N P H H S
C M A K E E A A C I E D U J Y E L L C U O P O I C E E
```

```
S V I K H N E F F E M A H O B A P A R I E V N R Y
Y L A A T S R I S J S M A T L F L M A T C I E U R
C N P L P O T S T M A L T M Z H A U H A U R R C W
N D R O C N E R H O W A D A G A N D I S E M E N S
Y F O N T E O N A G A M I S E E I H I D I D A T E
R T S F U N R N N Y R C H N T T R R A D B A V E C
N E U I C H E O M L I R C E U B M A H E R L O L A
O H O S N U N A M H I E E Y E O A M O R N N A N K
O T N D I I G O A F A R C A E N N E H F E F R A M
A E S A B O K J N O O G A G R O N R R A M R O Y O
E R R R E R M S A O A A R I S M A T I R A E O E I
T C C K I N G E N I C R U Y K R L A O T I N L U T
R J A M I A R T A O L I N U P A A E W S E C E K H
E H T O R C R A R C O A E M A S P G A A H C S A E
U C Z O H E I M C O P L R E I O R A C V L R A R R
M T A P E E M E O S N A R P L E E S A E Z S N E K
A R H P E R H O J N T U R G U S O N L D I C C N I
M G T T O N A H K I O N I N D L E A A V I N A G N
G A R E E N A L O G T O V E W I G R D E T N R J I
R T U G S H T G C N L H T N N A V D O R K E P R K
E E C H A E E O E I H N E E B O R R O E O S L E N
B N T N R L S L L I S O A I T O E L N R N T S S I
A G E O R O T A M G A W R J A S E E A A M E A P U
I N N V B E T E T E G E H Y P E V E G N A U R L O
K W A H N E H P S O R O R R M L T F R D E L A O M
```

```
G L L T A I S D C S E V R O I A I L S Y O A A O R
A E K C R I A L E P F F E F S A O R L A L R E N O
E A O N A A N E O E E O F L T M O B M N O O G A I
N T R E U A I A E A N R F U Y I L D O G T I F I T
B E R E S A L I S M U S I T R E U S T G E O T C A
E S G E T R I T S D I M N E C A C X R L D N A U O
G R P N I I L S M I N C M A H T A B S R C I T T R
A S I G A B F C U R C I T R O R L E L E A C A E R
L E D N A W S H M R I I C M O H S T P L K O I B E
F R G O H K I I M P L E S E L E U M E T M T W I O
F I R Z S N A T A O L H S T L I A H K C O D I M L
S N O N M I M K L M E T O L U E F T C R A L C U S
L A P S L L U T P M I R P S O E I U M R A M A R L
S S R U I R R E I A E R T I S S C A R L E O X O S
T P F O K E E D N N Y U H C I A L A S R N R D O C
O X O Y A N M E D T E S U L T A N U M I O E Y G S
S T K A I A R M O E N L T A L O G B E T A X A D R
D A F D N M E Y P A N M H C N B A A D R R E S T E
E R M E R A O L O E S R O P A L B O I A N Y A A I
T E I N D N A H P T G T A S C O I R U I U A W O A
E R R E D Y I R D E Y A H N E T E G M A E F I M U
N C I U A T L D B A E I R I H C V L I H L U A O T
S K T E A M M A N E L F R O G N I A R C A R A W T
G E O P N E C M E S A L A A H L O C A T R S A W T
I T L E V Y S C R H U R E L R A C E H I D R U U L
```

```
A H E R O O S P S R P R B W E E I S R R E S T O M
O I S H I N E S E A O A D M B R V F H O T P U A A
C R N R E K R I I I E B I D H C M R H N A L H N T
N I B C S T I A D M U S S T A H H L A D P T E O I
I U L Y I X I P A M O A E D R H T A R E I I S R M
S D E F O D T E T O T U G O F L I E N S C L C A A
H H S O P U L M T N S S G N R E C I T H A L I R N
S R I E K R G A P A I R O M W C I R E R T T E S T
L E W S T X A C C E F A H A A H A V G B H H A T T
G R O H D E I I P K N I E T I D R F S O X R I G I
A H D W R R I T D E O T G C V E R M I E E R S N G
T E I A V E O F E T R E H B R O I F D E I R E I O
S H W R R L W A E D I I O F W S U L S Y F E R D X
W O L O A M T E O A P E E E H H A B T A I V E O T
I R M T D L C N C R O R C I A R E V E R E T L R S
E R S E T A M I O T S E E H C D R I R K E A I O B
E R I L A B E C T T T O T S E I S E E R R T I X N
L D W I P H H H E C T D E S T L R A D R R L E A A
I N A A L D U E F M A I I H P L I L R A F O R P E
R A M I C H C E E T O O T S K O T M D G A A R D I
R H I W V R C T E U S S A A M H O Y U B E D E L E
S O E L D P R T P S D E O O I O R E O R A I C T W
N A S A L I D N N F E L N A E D W H E N A O Q A A R
I R L T O T C O N R A D I A L O G V A N X T R L R
E W W T D W A O H U V I D M R A E I W R M E M S N
```

Page 64

```
A U R G R G L M N D G I C L T I P O T L R U R A U
S E S C P R C O I S P S K C D P F A E F L O N U F
E E B E N I U M M E M N F O G E R G L N N I L P S
C A V N P E T C B R B T R U A U L C R A F L A N R
C P I O M C I E I A O A C L V T T G L I N S C D E
S I L P U A O F S L I S S A G F E R G S R E R E I
C G O T O U N N I I A C R C A L N P F N E D L L P
T H D T I O D S N C A P E K A B P T L S D C O I M
L L L L K O F N U O C C A E N C N G L S M N O S I
F A E E C A T T L T U L P E D T A O A C L L I T R
D F L E I L E S E T R A N N G K S L T K I N F C C
V C K D P K D S R E R O O T N S L E C T E O L E O
T U S V I C F C R N A V A M S M A M D C T L M E D
H G I T T A L F T A F F S O R K N V A R E S N R T
T S L E R S D P E K B S P E U N I A S I M L T L N
A G E E O P C M R C A F T T T A L O L A M I T C E
O L S R A L S A P B S A R E C K P B S T T F T E C
P C L S C E C N N E I L S L I U E F R E S R I U S
M U B A N C V D E O M L E R E A D A O G I S A C K
C L R O D L S L A E M A O T T T P T T N L C T D E
L P S R E N D I K R E M U E P A M R E I E T S S S
T S A V P A M N S U N D I T A P I C F L S S U O C
L O L A C E T A R I P K C R O L B C G E E T N O R
F O E G L S E M K C O C S I U L A R N R P N S I E
O D K E E T L N E D M P L N A F V O I F C G G M P
```

Page 66

```
E O G E R P A T A B T S T A B A I N G B R O E H D
E W N T A T S A T Y E H R N T R K G P O R O B G L
E A O M Z Y O B I P O P A S E C I E L L T M R G T
P T N R B A U T G E E I G N C R O S C A V K A R L
O U O A R T O R A M S L R Z B O P R A W E P W W S
D O S K B I R E A R F L A P Y T I F M O L R P P B
D R P E G E B R D I T O O A G R C Y E D C G A D C
G I T S W A M A M Z Z S U T E N T E S B R A S G O
G A S H C P N F E D L E G F L Y G O A E A F H Y I
E R S S U E S R H E P T D A N I T D C T T A T T A
O N C T C I D A B R R I K B G H R A E Y T W A R F
C T A C E P G E R S B I R B O B A D D D R D C P M
A D E A N O R A E W A G E S W D D A P S E A W E W
P R T C D A T B R P Y F C T H A Y T O S O T E A E
R T B E A M A B S A B A O N S B D G U T B W C P A
F B O E N H S U M S I S H O A R E R C A A E A N C
O U E T K E D R A H L A I F R V U U A P P B I N N
S A S L D S E Y R S E R Y O A R N A F F S N F E D
Y R F A R A W I N G K A E L K C U Y I U L E G M V
Z T T L P I N G G F R B E A R O B U N G C A E T T
A S R W E A G B A F L D T C T N C R E G V R G R O
P E N W A P N I K S T G R I G G V A N O E C S H W
R R P O E G N U E L Z A T B U E R N E T Z C A S N
S E B T I N G N N R Z I F O O M Z E S E R B O R I
W O R F T A P I T A D O T E R R P H A N G B A O R
```

Page 68

```
O L M G K A G E R O C B W C H A L T W A L A Y D D
I L T T E N S K B O W H H L O I R D N A T D M R A
D R A L E S E S L R M T E E C N R C A R R K R E A
G B L A O N A W K O N R A C R S R A A T E L O A M
S M E E T K S T A T U M E N R F A N R E O F B O N
G D T B O O U R N E R E C L A A I C C A O C M R S
S U N D R D P E D G A L R E R H S S A B O G E L H
T P A A A W B R I B A R U P P O J I R E T A O E G
W E M P P M R A N U C A A A R E Y R G L A M K U M
L R T I I T H N D R K R Y R M R D R A L N B I A E
Y E A T D W A U O R G P A E D T P H O K R B N H A
R W B B H O K P R H O T E S G E O E B K C A S R A
A R Y A O R T E G M A L T W A A O S P L A C F E I
L A E S R T E E G B D E A S S R I K E B L A S E R
E O P E W S T R C L R R M D R O H R L A E L O E B
D W D E E A R R E E T I L R C D R O R I F L A T R
D E R T H K M E R F H G D B E C T W E M O A R A K
W B D A K B L N R R T W A E A I B K F T D B R R E
E E L T O I G U S K R O H H U D H R A C S E H Y D
U G L B J O Y B R U L W F B D U E R R T T S A A W
D S N O G E D A M A P L G B O A I R C B O N B S E
M E W T E H C L E C B T A A D O T K H A H E A G A
N O L T C K T E S B M D W D Y A O H D A C Y G I O
B S K O K M A R S E K R A U G L S F B M O N T J E
A A E M E A I O F D R A B K N R E W U D R R H R A
```

Page 69

```
E U E E A N G R P U B F T E N A S H T U O S A I N
E R D R R A H R E B L O H E C D U J D R O M A A A
V U D O C T I C T O I C I C I T B I Y A Z T A N Z
E D E M I S U N O A S U H O N U O R U M Q U E A U
P O G N E N N E M E A P T X G O R U B B I L E R I
A C A R R T A E A D N G O S E D P N D P I A G E O
A P L E O P Y G R P A N L A L A I N I O E B C P E
E I A E N O F O I N P E U Y O A R E G I Q O N U B
I T I N G E R A A C I L M N A G A M E H C A I I L
R A N E K G D E Y N S G I I M M B B E T T F O C E
U A K B N I M A F E K R W A N I A I O O H A N N A
A M A B A B B N D A N M A A D Z B R G C E W A A C
Q E E R T I A N U S F A I R E S W E N O O S T K O
U O R I I C N A I D A D G A L S L R I A O B O U R
A T Q A R E E P L A G A S C L E L E R B A P N R A
B I A L G B C C S M E N E S E Y I B N G A U O S H
M S O R U I N U S O A L S A H C I I R G B T H A C
A A M O O G E A W T M I T O C O V I B N I I R F I
Z G C C T O L R I N L A N O Y R A W B L F C I A Z
O S O A I S U L A Y O S T E M A L A U I C A S W I
R M D A R E I R U V B I U N I S O S P C I D N A L
O A A H L G T I A M A N G M A I A A E A R F J C E
M E N C A B U N U I C E A E C V A F R N O A R T N
O C I U G S O S A S S I B R O O N D E R O L A A K
B Z A E O G A L I B Y A B U R K I W N U G A N D C
```

Page 70

```
C R O F Z Y I O R N I T A L P E L M I A I T I O C
B I U L U G C I S U M N C T C C I D N M R P I R H
N N I U U I I U B U R M S M I Z N O L M Y R M O M
B E R E M U T O R E U A E C N S E L E R C U M U I
O C U P R I O U E S I L N O A R I N M U U N Y I R
N I I R A M N M N A G M I N D O N D N H T I O S M
G N Z C B U M U I N N A X E A R O I R E R L D I U
I S S O N I N O H I M T N U U I C L S U R C P T O
M L G F D C K E I L U M U I M E R A C M L I Y R N
E A D R S C O L N A I U B R O N M N E U M E N K I
L L I U M O P S S O M D Y O M I A G S I N H U M M
A M U I A T R R T M C A H H B R O R N O S E K Z I
P R O S S A I L E I P A L Y O G L O N E E G P N N
U N F I O I A R A N I I S D R E H N N O L L N O S
E I U L D I A T D M U I L S I N C I R N M O M G G
E T M A C N E U I M L S I A L R A U S U U I N R E
A M U U R N M M I R A R C I V O R D I S I H O A N
U E C F L E I N N S C B O N E O S I A P N O R T I
G R C S U G O R U I O N N N R E E N D T A B U R O
A I C I U Y X A N C I H C S U B I L G I T D I I G
M P H O M U I R I U M N C I L D C A I C O M O R E
U R E S G O R T T Y U K R D E A P X N P P N N O N
S O H P M L U C O B A L T S E L E M M E R C I H U
O M F Y M D G L I I U M U I R O N I D S G P C E L
I I A E I I I E T H C I O I M R M U B T M A M U I
```

Page 71

```
N Y M I P H A G U S C N A P A N E R N A T L E U C
L A M N O S R A A I R C A L F F S E D I L C A O L
Y S U A D E O T N I E M L C P C N G U N P P R W I
S E N E T T M R E P A T D R R S I S K C T S I V A
T E M Y S Y S T E C S Y E T S Y F E S O T N E I U
A B A V E K A W M U N E A E R R E T R U T E Y E C
L O O I T O X N C E R U N R U F S U A B A L E F S
E L L N S H Y L H E U M S D M E S H R L S H L X N
A R T S E D C C L E K A I N N A N L U H S E A R Y
V E E B G I C O C E B R A Y B U O B E H L O K F B
U E A R N X N Y R A H K P L L T T L R I F S H F C
C U O B R N R M A D P N T C E D O N T L R V E R A
I T D S D V E H E P A E H H B M P H S O M I H D N
S O O F E Q U E O A R R C E S Y L P E N E L A N O
T E L T T S E R A S T R A A T A Y E L S K E L E T
N E P F A G F O R R A S E M R N R I V P L C O N O
H E S B D V K L E Y E H R T N A D S A P E M L R B
N L E C A A N E A M S N E D L S A M S C G V L A T
E O I W L A H H D L G L A D S E C A S A E S N E N
S K G S Y A P A F U N B I M X N B F B P I L L M O
E S L E D I H R B A L L N D I T L C C A M R A B D
M O B K E H G A S G P P E C X N A D D C H Y B A V
M W N C A N M S E R A M E T I R C H E R D O Y O W
A T U O B A E I N T N I Y S C S U L A A M A C H D
L H T M T R H T S E T N S Y R O T A N A O T S Y S
```

Page 72

```
O Y R H C U F C U L S U S M O L E C E H C A E V I
T O Q S I Y R H M U G T C M Y D U L N I R A P O L
A R I E A T R E L L P E A C E N U B B U A M Y R R
I L L N R N S E B R O L R E R U G R U Q A Y T N Z
L Y E A R E G I W A A A I T E L R A O D C A I U M
T H O G R E E M E H T W H S O E U S V E L F R R E
N A R A Y U W R A Y E M O E R A N T I E E O C O A
L M O N Y R N G C U V R G A M N A U O U R A H C L
E A L E I A U A H A M N I I B R N A T E E R A R T
Z A A P R B B R E U I N D R E A Z I G S A N A M L
U H B L A S U T R S E E N I R E P E A I E N C R B
D A Z S A B R O P O C L K W I E Y G R O D R A R V
A U S T L N N T A R M C T E N I E N A R I O L E L
R M S A R G E L L A U A A G T A L D W M N I V T E
E D I A D S H L M O N N O A W O L O R E A D L O T
I S L R C G S A L R R E E M S E A L O W L O L G A
L V E R E G P M F W A R I L E T T F N I R E A M L
T U P A C G O H E F Y K L A W T N A R O C N L D S
Q R O T L M R I R W N C O C R Y O V Y W E N A R E
U T Y R T I L W G O B L A L P Q S Y D A M I L H M
O P U R E R L E D R Y I C C O R E A M S E C R E E
I A Z S M C E U M B U U K I T H S J E E A N E D I
S E A O I R L B A R I A P R L T A E A D C Y A N E
E T B N I V O M O O M E E L P B A Z J I R E N A V
N L D L T Y R C N S N E C A R R O N E S E C L L R
```

Page 73

```
B T N A H P E L R L A N A L O D O K C P E I S H L
O H A P I U G E E L E T H P H K E L O C A F Y L L
A T T N N E N P P O R N I Y S C R I D W P M U A E
N N Y P E P E Z H R R A A B A U O C O O P A S W J
N A O W A R L A I R O N O O B A N A M P O T W N F
M R O R A E L G L B R P O S O T E O N P I H T E A
A K O M O D R A C A T K E T E E L U R C W N E F T
D I R O D O T G P R H A N R I C E M A H O L A F F
L L L N T R N O L A T E S R E H U J U P E F F U U
O O G G O I N A D O T L L R K C E A G S O R A E B
T H M W I H A E C E R T W O O D P A K C I I G L A
R H C E S E U G I H S G R N R T S T R I O R P O R
A I U S A V E R N T G M T O A G N O E C T T H O B
W D P B E R C U A H S A L M E K A C E M P Y A N E
F N O T C O I P P R C H P A E M O E A L L E T R A
L A A G O P W I N E I I M N Z S B Y B E A N I M O
A M I N E S C T E R N E R H C A O P A B W E R Y N
A E A F S P L I W W D E E N A N O I E S R V C E K
T T N A I O A D A L R U S A I H R L A O N L H E E
E R A T P P T Y S T R K R C N I N O E D W O H A T
O N G U O R G P U V A E L I O C E O M R A L L I G
R A L L K A O R R D S P E A A N R C C A P O E L A
C O Y B S L L I A Y A L W S R W O F C L A A O O T
S A O P B O A N A R E A M E G H S N O A F R W R O
A E T A C B I E T E D N A L L A E I S N E N N A T
```

Page 74

```
L P A I C K B R Y R E G N A R O A C C G L N O A H
A N T N A L E R A U R W A R R N S N H I I L P O O
O N D G E B E M A H E T C T O R S E K C N G M S N
M L S G T N P B U R G L E A A T P R O L E D U L A
L A H P L A R I O L E E T A L Y I M A N E W O E R
O E C I A T O C N A M R E W A R R L E A R Q L F I
O Y T W D B Y I R P S T T P E N E D Z T E C A U L
G U R D N N I S A D L E L E L P B L E P R O B E R
T N Z S A I U E L I S M E R U S A R K E E L S T I
O A U C C H Q T L A A O O R B A N C A P N A B W O
S S S E T S A L P K I N T I T P M U F F I N E A R
H O I T R P W N M I C A C H R N I E N A G H R R T
B R C S I E T U U L A F A I A I S H C P S E I Y S
S L E E N E A T P A F S T O A G L I Q N N T T E N
C U S L G R O L H L E I P U S E A D A E T P P A I
N A M O A L S L T E A P P A S H S W I T A L C B P
K C U R E L M A E E I E L U M E M T O E Y E H E E
U A C E E D A M E E N P I E F O L I T R R R A E S
G L B T L L B E R C W O K E R C C A S F B E B S H
A P A O N N U I T T B R A T Y R O R B C E U L G R
N A N N E F R E U A R I C S Y R T A E M A A P M I
T Q U I R E P R A S S N P U O E B A L L Y E K R U
L A G N R M A K S E B E E C U B N C O W U T L P T
A S N A P G R R T N U A W A R S A R L O A L A O Y
T U N A E U L A U R H L E M T H M A L M E M T T R
```

Page 75

```
A A C A N O R E L E C S A L S I N I S N Y A C N R A H O T
I S C A Y O N Z N R A D N R T E C G S D N A H I E H A K S
B E N Y S N L I O L S D C A Y C A R I N N E J E F S A O P
H Y L H E B A S A C B A E V R N N K V A L L O L S G N I R
E D A S Q H N D A S V L R O B O Y N O A S I S H U K C A L
S B I O U A B E C A L S N M E S O E T O L L E Y A C A N B
E A L A E L G N D S S N I I H L N Y S W A L E R T L C Y O
Y H A K A V I B D S E T A T E N G S G A V W A R A T S E N
E D O S P A D S A E N N U O E A U C O D N I D S P F O R O
L N E H G L E S K O V N I M E D A U H C A B U K E D E T F
L A N E R C M O L L C A C N P U L Y A I V O K V T R I H E
A K K V C I P M Y E L T N I P N A P L M E L L A T I F A G
V A E E S E A S E V B A Y B I N C Y R U Y E L G G R H N U
H T D E E R O O A V R E I R S E L O S E V O A E R A N N I
O E S M R E R O S E R C C A L G D U N G A Y C I D N O O S
N A Y E A O A D E M D A A R C S A N E S H O S M C A N N C
L C T I G E E O A T E P T E A A S A R A L C R E D A Y I I
O V C O N T H N I N U I R R K E T I K N K E G R W N O E N
I I K E L A E F E L O T M L A N D D N A A L N A O S D K A
A W A H S T R L E R M Y K B L D S N I S S L A D O B R O I
I N T M M L G U A E I O C G E A T O G R T E R R O I G J F
C H E A O M D E N A L R N S Y B E T I L E S R R E T A N R
R A S I K K I N S N N Y O A G S I D A S M E D A W A Y M W
E N D E Y M A G S C A N S O R A N N B O O U A H C R A A L
G R R Y U O C A D I A R A M E B G A R G T N C L Y R M M C
O E T S N T R E T R E S E I A T C N I A R A S C T D O O U
G A R N I A O L I E T O R L O T I R N S H C S A O H T D R
S T D U S E Y S I M A F N E R C E E I A T N D G R C A V E
A N D N E L A A I N G T H E A O R A U G R O E U T W U N H
```

Page 78

2	6	4	7	1	3	5	8	9
1	7	8	5	6	9	4	3	2
3	5	9	8	2	4	1	7	6
5	8	6	2	9	7	3	1	4
9	4	1	3	8	6	7	2	5
7	2	3	4	5	1	9	6	8
4	1	2	9	7	8	6	5	3
6	3	5	1	4	2	8	9	7
8	9	7	6	3	5	2	4	1

Page 79

4	3	7	9	1	6	2	8	5
2	6	1	5	8	4	9	3	7
5	9	8	3	2	7	4	1	6
8	4	6	1	9	2	7	5	3
1	5	9	7	3	8	6	4	2
3	7	2	4	6	5	8	9	1
9	8	5	2	7	1	3	6	4
7	1	3	6	4	9	5	2	8
6	2	4	8	5	3	1	7	9

Page 80

5	9	8	7	2	1	3	4	6
4	1	3	6	8	9	7	2	5
2	7	6	4	5	3	1	8	9
7	6	9	5	3	2	8	1	4
8	2	4	1	6	7	9	5	3
1	3	5	9	4	8	2	6	7
9	5	7	2	1	4	6	3	8
3	4	1	8	9	6	5	7	2
6	8	2	3	7	5	4	9	1

Page 81

5	8	2	9	7	3	6	1	4
7	9	3	6	4	1	5	8	2
6	4	1	2	8	5	3	9	7
9	5	8	7	2	4	1	6	3
1	2	4	3	9	6	7	5	8
3	7	6	5	1	8	4	2	9
8	6	9	1	3	7	2	4	5
4	3	5	8	6	2	9	7	1
2	1	7	4	5	9	8	3	6

Page 82

2	5	3	6	1	8	4	9	7
8	7	9	3	4	2	6	1	5
1	6	4	9	5	7	2	8	3
9	1	2	4	3	5	7	6	8
6	4	7	2	8	9	5	3	1
5	3	8	7	6	1	9	4	2
4	8	5	1	7	6	3	2	9
3	2	1	5	9	4	8	7	6
7	9	6	8	2	3	1	5	4

Page 83

1	8	4	3	6	9	7	2	5
3	5	2	8	4	7	9	6	1
6	9	7	5	2	1	8	4	3
2	1	5	4	8	3	6	7	9
9	4	6	2	7	5	3	1	8
7	3	8	1	9	6	2	5	4
8	6	1	9	5	2	4	3	7
5	2	9	7	3	4	1	8	6
4	7	3	6	1	8	5	9	2

Page 84

4	7	8	5	2	9	1	3	6
1	3	6	4	7	8	2	9	5
9	5	2	6	3	1	4	7	8
5	9	3	2	8	7	6	1	4
8	2	7	1	6	4	9	5	3
6	1	4	3	9	5	7	8	2
7	6	9	8	4	3	5	2	1
3	4	5	7	1	2	8	6	9
2	8	1	9	5	6	3	4	7

Page 85

3	6	9	8	1	5	7	4	2
8	1	4	2	7	9	5	6	3
2	7	5	4	6	3	9	8	1
5	9	1	7	4	2	6	3	8
7	2	8	6	3	1	4	9	5
6	4	3	9	5	8	2	1	7
4	5	2	1	8	6	3	7	9
9	8	7	3	2	4	1	5	6
1	3	6	5	9	7	8	2	4

Page 86

2	6	8	5	1	7	9	4	3
1	3	7	4	9	2	8	5	6
9	4	5	8	3	6	2	7	1
6	9	1	2	8	5	4	3	7
4	8	2	7	6	3	1	9	5
5	7	3	1	4	9	6	8	2
3	1	4	6	7	8	5	2	9
7	5	6	9	2	4	3	1	8
8	2	9	3	5	1	7	6	4

Page 87

7	2	6	5	3	8	4	9	1
3	9	4	6	1	7	8	5	2
1	5	8	2	9	4	6	7	3
9	8	2	1	4	3	7	6	5
6	7	1	9	8	5	3	2	4
4	3	5	7	6	2	9	1	8
5	4	9	3	7	1	2	8	6
2	6	3	8	5	9	1	4	7
8	1	7	4	2	6	5	3	9

E	M	S	O	J	Y	A	R	C
C	R	O	A	S	E	J	M	Y
A	Y	J	C	M	R	O	S	E
J	E	R	Y	C	S	M	O	A
S	O	C	R	A	M	E	Y	J
M	A	Y	J	E	O	R	C	S
O	S	A	M	Y	J	C	E	R
Y	C	M	E	R	A	S	J	O
R	J	E	S	O	C	Y	A	M

2	3	7	4	5	9	1	8	6
4	8	9	2	6	1	3	5	7
1	5	6	8	7	3	4	9	2
5	1	4	6	8	7	2	3	9
3	6	8	5	9	2	7	4	1
9	7	2	1	3	4	8	6	5
8	2	3	9	1	5	6	7	4
6	4	5	7	2	8	9	1	3
7	9	1	3	4	6	5	2	8

R	K	O	T	W	A	F	L	E
W	L	E	K	F	O	T	A	R
A	F	T	R	E	L	O	K	W
O	R	A	L	K	F	W	E	T
K	W	L	E	T	R	A	O	F
T	E	F	O	A	W	K	R	L
F	T	K	A	L	E	R	W	O
L	O	W	F	R	K	E	T	A
E	A	R	W	O	T	L	F	K

<u>N</u> <u>I</u> <u>T</u> <u>R</u> <u>A</u> <u>T</u> <u>E</u>

S	E	C	T	N	A	O	R	I
O	A	R	E	I	C	N	T	S
I	N	T	O	S	R	A	C	E
E	I	A	C	O	N	R	S	T
R	S	O	A	T	I	E	N	C
C	T	N	R	E	S	I	A	O
N	R	I	S	C	O	T	E	A
A	C	E	I	R	T	S	O	N
T	O	S	N	A	E	C	I	R

Page 92

6	2	5	7	4	1	8	3	9
8	4	9	2	3	6	1	7	5
1	3	7	8	5	9	4	6	2
2	8	6	3	1	5	9	4	7
9	5	1	4	7	8	3	2	6
3	7	4	9	6	2	5	8	1
4	6	2	1	9	3	7	5	8
7	9	8	5	2	4	6	1	3
5	1	3	6	8	7	2	9	4

Page 93

4	7	1	2	6	9	8	5	3
6	5	2	8	7	3	9	4	1
9	8	3	5	1	4	2	6	7
3	1	8	9	4	5	6	7	2
5	6	4	7	2	1	3	9	8
2	9	7	6	3	8	5	1	4
1	2	9	4	8	6	7	3	5
8	3	5	1	9	7	4	2	6
7	4	6	3	5	2	1	8	9

Page 94

8	9	3	2	4	6	7	5	1
1	5	2	7	3	9	4	8	6
6	4	7	8	1	5	2	9	3
3	6	1	9	7	8	5	2	4
4	8	5	3	2	1	9	6	7
7	2	9	5	6	4	1	3	8
2	7	4	6	9	3	8	1	5
9	3	8	1	5	7	6	4	2
5	1	6	4	8	2	3	7	9

Page 95

8	6	5	9	3	7	2	4	1
9	1	7	2	4	8	5	6	3
3	2	4	6	1	5	7	9	8
2	5	9	4	7	1	8	3	6
7	4	6	3	8	9	1	5	2
1	8	3	5	2	6	4	7	9
5	3	2	1	9	4	6	8	7
6	7	1	8	5	3	9	2	4
4	9	8	7	6	2	3	1	5

Page 96

5	2	4	6	9	7	8	3	1
7	3	8	2	1	4	9	5	6
1	6	9	3	5	8	4	7	2
6	1	3	4	7	9	2	8	5
9	8	2	1	6	5	3	4	7
4	7	5	8	3	2	6	1	9
8	4	6	5	2	1	7	9	3
2	5	7	9	4	3	1	6	8
3	9	1	7	8	6	5	2	4

Page 97

8	5	3	9	1	6	4	2	7
7	9	1	2	4	3	5	6	8
2	6	4	5	8	7	9	3	1
5	1	8	4	6	9	3	7	2
9	7	2	8	3	1	6	5	4
4	3	6	7	5	2	8	1	9
3	2	7	6	9	4	1	8	5
1	8	9	3	2	5	7	4	6
6	4	5	1	7	8	2	9	3

Page 98

8	2	5	7	6	1	9	3	4
1	3	4	2	5	9	7	8	6
9	7	6	8	3	4	2	1	5
4	5	9	1	8	6	3	2	7
6	1	3	4	2	7	8	5	9
2	8	7	3	9	5	4	6	1
3	9	1	5	4	2	6	7	8
5	6	2	9	7	8	1	4	3
7	4	8	6	1	3	5	9	2

Page 99

5	4	6	1	8	7	9	3	2
9	8	2	4	5	3	6	7	1
3	1	7	2	9	6	4	8	5
7	2	8	9	1	4	3	5	6
1	6	5	8	3	2	7	4	9
4	3	9	6	7	5	1	2	8
8	9	3	5	4	1	2	6	7
2	7	1	3	6	8	5	9	4
6	5	4	7	2	9	8	1	3

Page 102

×180 9	4	×126 7	+24 6	8	2	1	3	5
8	5	9	2	7	×72 3	4	6	1
×42 3	7	2	+11 5	6	1	8	+27 4	9
×42 1	6	-2 5	7	×216 4	9	3	8	2
7	1	8	+21 3	9	6	5	2	4
×15 5	3	4	8	1	×420 7	2	-3 9	6
+17 6	9	3	×6 1	2	4	×35 7	5	8
2	8	-2 6	4	3	5	×504 9	1	7
+24 4	2	1	9	+28 5	8	6	×21 7	3

Page 103

×27 3	9	+21 5	6	+10 1	7	2	8	+4 4
×360 9	5	4	2	8	3	+30 7	6	1
8	6	2	×180 5	3	1	4	9	7
+22 7	3	+25 9	8	4	+21 2	6	1	5
6	+9 2	7	4	9	8	+15 1	×135 5	3
-2 2	×168 7	3	1	5	6	+2 8	4	9
4	1	8	+24 3	2	5	+22 9	7	6
+15 1	8	6	×63 9	7	4	×45 5	3	2
×20 5	4	1	×1512 7	6	9	3	×32 2	8

Page 104

+17 2	+13 5	8	+18 7	1	4	×162 6	3	9
4	2	5	1	6	×189 9	3	×56 8	7
9	+18 4	2	6	3	7	-3 8	5	1
+20 7	9	4	+24 3	8	-4 1	5	+14 2	6
×378 1	7	9	8	5	×48 6	2	4	3
×864 8	3	6	+15 4	9	+13 5	7	1	2
6	1	7	5	2	3	+13 4	9	8
3	6	1	2	4	8	×315 9	7	5
+26 5	8	3	9	+20 7	2	1	×24 6	4

Page 105

-3 9	6	+22 7	8	2	4	+12 5	1	3
+27 5	2	8	6	9	1	+18 4	3	×280 7
4	9	×648 6	2	5	3	1	7	8
8	3	4	1	+9 7	2	6	9	5
+17 2	8	×252 3	7	6	+21 5	9	4	1
1	5	2	9	4	7	+28 3	8	6
3	4	×1620 9	5	1	8	7	+3 6	2
-1 6	7	1	3	-1 8	9	2	5	×36 4
+20 7	1	5	4	3	×96 6	8	2	9

Page 106

×2160 8	6	×80 5	2	×63 7	9	1	+7 4	3
9	5	8	3	+16 6	2	7	1	×960 4
+19 7	4	1	+8 5	3	6	×144 2	9	8
1	3	4	×504 6	2	7	9	8	5
4	2	+21 3	7	9	+23 1	8	5	6
+20 3	9	2	×128 1	8	4	+25 5	6	7
×10 2	8	9	4	+22 5	3	6	7	+2 1
5	7	6	+18 9	1	8	4	3	2
+27 6	1	7	8	+16 4	5	3	×18 2	9

Page 107

+12 2	7	+23 6	9	8	+15 3	5	1	×864 4
3	×4320 8	7	×32 1	2	4	6	5	9
8	6	5	4	7	+20 2	1	9	3
-5 6	1	9	2	×1120 5	7	4	3	8
×108 9	3	+12 2	6	4	1	8	7	5
4	×336 2	8	×1215 5	3	9	+29 7	6	1
1	4	3	7	9	×10 5	2	8	6
+12 7	5	1	+17 3	6	8	9	×112 4	2
+14 5	9	×32 4	8	1	×162 6	3	2	7

Page 108

×28 4	7	+25 2	8	×720 5	3	1	9	6
1	5	6	9	2	4	+24 8	7	3
3	9	×10 5	-6 1	7	6	×1260 4	+27 8	2
7	3	1	2	4	9	5	6	8
×60 5	4	×144 8	6	1	7	2	3	9
×864 8	2	3	7	×864 6	1	9	-1 5	4
9	6	×3780 4	5	3	8	+9 7	2	×35 1
+24 2	1	9	3	8	×360 5	6	4	7
6	8	7	×1728 4	9	2	3	1	5

Page 109

×11340 9	5	×30 6	1	×96 3	2	4	8	7
7	6	1	5	4	×3888 9	8	3	2
6	4	×24 8	3	2	5	9	+17 7	1
×84 3	7	×1512 2	9	6	8	1	5	4
4	2	-2 9	7	+12 1	3	+11 5	6	8
×144 8	9	7	2	5	×504 4	6	1	3
2	1	5	+19 6	8	7	3	×1728 4	9
-4 1	8	3	-5 4	9	6	7	2	5
5	+23 3	4	8	×84 7	1	2	×270 9	6

Page 110

×280 5	7	8	×72 3	4	6	9	+8 1	2
+28 3	6	+17 9	1	+30 2	4	7	8	5
4	8	3	2	7	9	-4 1	5	6
7	3	2	+31 6	8	1	×180 5	4	9
×12 1	4	-1 7	8	5	+24 2	6	9	+11 3
+22 6	1	5	×1440 4	9	8	3	2	7
8	2	6	9	3	5	4	7	1
×360 2	+25 9	1	+22 5	6	7	8	-1 3	4
9	5	4	7	1	-1 3	2	×48 6	8

Page 111

1	×36 9	4	8	×180 5	3	2	7	6
+19 7	8	+21 2	5	1	6	9	+7 3	4
4	7	5	-3 3	6	+21 9	1	2	8
×216 9	×42 6	7	+22 4	2	5	3	8	1
3	+21 5	9	+12 1	7	4	×4608 8	6	2
8	4	3	2	9	1	6	-2 5	7
-1 2	3	+14 1	6	+15 4	8	×1575 7	9	5
+22 6	1	8	7	3	2	5	-5 4	9
5	2	×3024 6	9	8	7	×12 4	1	3

Page 112

7	9	+22 2	4	8	×1680 1	6	×405 3	5
×32 4	+16 1	3	6	2	5	7	8	9
1	8	4	+14 5	7	2	9	6	3
8	+6 6	1	2	×3402 9	7	3	×120 5	4
2	+12 7	5	×9 3	1	+34 4	8	9	6
+18 6	5	×392 8	7	3	9	4	-1 2	1
9	3	7	+7 1	6	8	+9 5	4	2
+23 3	4	9	+19 8	5	6	×28 2	1	7
5	2	6	9	×12 4	3	1	×56 7	8

Page 113

-2 2	4	×378 6	7	9	×5 5	1	+25 8	3
3	8	1	×360 9	5	2	7	6	4
-1 6	7	×360 5	3	4	8	×108 2	9	1
×35 7	5	3	8	×1152 6	1	4	2	9
×36 1	9	2	+12 4	8	6	+20 3	5	7
×36 9	2	4	6	×112 1	7	8	3	5
4	×5040 6	7	5	2	+17 3	9	+14 1	8
8	1	9	×6 2	3	4	5	-1 7	6
+25 5	3	8	1	×6048 7	9	6	4	2

×54 9	3	×70 7	2	+26 6	8	1	+16 4	5
1	2	5	×2160 6	3	9	8	7	4
×2520 5	1	3	8	9	7	+13 4	6	2
6	7	8	5	+6 4	2	3	+9 1	9
3	×360 5	9	4	×420 7	6	2	+8 8	1
4	8	+22 2	9	1	5	×756 7	3	6
+17 2	×4 4	1	7	5	3	6	9	8
7	×648 9	6	1	8	4	5	×42 2	3
8	6	4	3	+21 2	1	9	5	7

8	+14 5	+25 9	7	1	+16 4	3	×96 2	6
5	9	4	2	7	3	6	8	1
9	×48 4	3	8	+18 2	6	1	×4480 5	7
×864 3	6	1	×14 9	5	7	2	4	8
7	2	8	6	+17 3	5	9	1	4
+8 6	1	7	4	9	+27 2	8	3	5
1	×294 7	2	3	×32 4	8	5	+22 6	9
×24 4	3	+19 6	5	8	1	×63 7	9	2
2	-3 8	5	×216 1	6	9	4	7	3

+9 5	4	1	+25 9	7	×12 2	6	+17 8	3
+11 8	×126 2	7	×40 5	9	1	×144 4	3	6
3	1	9	8	5	7	2	6	4
+16 2	5	×12 3	4	+22 6	8	×252 9	1	7
9	-4 6	2	×28 7	1	4	3	×40 5	8
+11 7	+30 3	4	×288 1	2	6	8	×45 9	5
4	9	8	6	3	×280 5	7	2	1
-1 6	7	+19 5	3	8	9	1	4	2
+8 1	8	+24 6	2	4	3	+12 5	7	9

+19 6	9	8	×12 4	1	3	+26 2	5	7
4	1	5	2	3	8	9	×2352 7	6
×15 5	4	+13 1	7	2	9	6	3	8
3	7	-6 2	8	6	+5 4	×4320 5	9	1
+20 7	2	+26 3	6	9	1	4	8	-4 5
×5 1	5	4	3	7	+14 6	8	2	9
+28 2	3	×2520 7	9	8	+5 5	1	+15 6	4
8	6	9	5	+6 4	2	7	1	3
9	×48 8	6	+13 1	5	7	+8 3	4	2

Page 118

-3 5	×288 2	1	8	+21 6	3	4	7	9
8	4	2	×63 9	7	1	×90 5	3	6
+22 3	6	9	1	+25 4	8	7	+17 5	2
6	8	5	+11 7	1	4	+19 9	2	3
+18 9	5	+18 4	6	3	2	8	1	7
4	1	3	5	×315 9	7	×96 2	6	8
7	9	×480 8	3	2	5	6	4	1
1	7	6	2	5	×162 9	3	8	×20 4
×1008 2	3	7	4	-2 8	6	+23 1	9	5

Page 119

+11 1	3	9	8	5	2	×84 4	7	6
7	+9 9	1	+30 4	8	5	3	+23 6	2
4	5	+18 8	6	7	×324 1	2	3	9
9	×320 4	3	5	2	6	×1344 8	1	7
8	2	5	+8 7	1	9	6	4	×60 3
+20 6	×28 1	7	×2592 3	4	8	+18 9	2	5
5	6	2	1	9	3	7	8	4
3	×224 8	4	2	-1 6	7	+27 5	9	1
2	7	-3 6	9	+8 3	4	1	5	8

Page 120

-4 5	9	×56 7	4	2	-5 6	1	×2160 8	3
-5 2	7	+3 1	3	×32 8	4	9	5	6
×40 4	5	2	+16 7	3	9	-2 8	6	1
+11 3	2	+14 8	1	6	×35 7	5	4	9
6	8	5	+16 9	4	1	+9 2	3	7
×84 7	4	3	2	1	×2160 5	6	9	×40 8
1	3	6	×2160 8	9	2	4	7	5
-7 8	1	9	6	5	3	7	×16 2	4
×9720 9	6	4	5	+21 7	8	3	1	2

Page 121

×6 2	3	9	+26 7	4	6	8	1	5
+32 4	9	6	8	×5 1	5	+23 3	7	2
6	7	8	4	+13 5	3	1	2	9
7	×2880 5	2	9	8	4	6	+3 3	1
9	1	7	-4 2	6	×1728 8	4	+20 5	3
+8 1	6	5	3	+9 7	2	9	8	4
3	×60 4	1	5	+16 9	7	+8 2	6	8
8	2	-2 4	6	3	×45 1	5	9	7
+15 5	8	×6 3	1	2	9	×1176 7	4	6

Page 122

+15 7	5	3	×1296 8	6	9	1	+14 4	2
×864 1	6	2	3	9	×200 5	4	×7560 7	8
9	8	1	×21 7	3	2	5	6	4
+20 8	1	6	×120 5	×28 4	7	-1 3	2	9
+15 3	4	9	6	7	1	2	×72 8	5
5	3	4	1	×96 2	8	6	9	×126 7
4	9	8	2	5	×42 6	7	1	3
+26 2	7	×450 5	9	1	4	+26 8	3	6
6	+9 2	7	+19 4	8	3	9	5	1

Page 126

Clues across top: 6↓ 10↓ 32↓ 22↓ ... 39↓ 17↓

- 11→ 1 2 3 5 | 17→ 8 9
- 29→ 5 8 7 9 | 4↓ | 16→ 3 5 8 | 6↓
- 17→ 9 8 | 7→ 2 1 4 | 17↓
- 39↓ 13→ 5 8 | 9→ 8 1 | 15→ 6 9
- 45→ 6 4 5 2 9 3 1 7 8
- 16→ 9 7 | 4→ 1 3 | 16→ 7 9 | 20↓
- 20→ 9 8 3 | 12→ 9 3 | 14↓ 4↓
- 16↓ 24→ 9 8 7 | 24→ 8 4 9 3
- 13→ 7 6 | 11→ 3 2 5 1

Page 127

Clues: 8↓ 16↓ ... 22↓ 15↓

- 16→ 7 9 | 16→ 9 7
- 7→ 1 4 2 | 3↓ | 23↓ 24→ 9 7 8
- 6→ 3 1 2 | 15↓ | 34↓ 21→ 7 8 6
- 24→ 5 4 9 6 | 7↓
- 7→ 1 2 4
- 7↓ 14→ 2 3 1 8
- 6↓ 8→ 3 1 4 | 19→ 6 9 4 | 10↓ 7↓ | 7↓
- 4↓ 7→ 1 2 4 | 7→ 1 2 4
- 4→ 3 1 | 4→ 1 3

Page 128

Clues: 3↓ 4↓ 16↓ 9↓ ... 23↓ 4↓

- 11→ 1 3 2 5 | 4→ 1 3
- 10→ 2 1 4 3 | 6↓ | 7→ 2 4 1
- 4→ 3 1 | 8→ 1 4 3 | 7↓ | 4↓
- 39↓ 5→ 4 1 | 3→ 1 2 | 16↓ 5→ 2 3 | 33↓
- 11↓ 45→ 2 9 6 8 7 4 3 5 1 | 24↓
- 16→ 9 7 | 17→ 9 8 | 17→ 9 8 | 21↓
- 10↓ 24→ 8 9 7 | 16→ 9 7 | 17↓ 16↓
- 4↓ 10→ 3 6 1 | 29→ 5 8 9 7
- 6→ 1 5 | 30→ 7 6 8 9

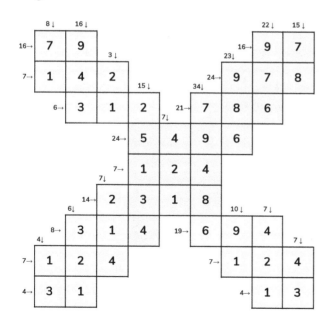

Page 129

Page 130

Page 131

Page 132

Page 133

```
              14↓  17↓                  11↓  16↓  8↓
         17→   8    9              23→   8    9    6
  13↓ 31↓                    6↓ 19↓
45→  5    1    6    8    4    9    3    7    2
17→  8    9         3→   2    1         11↓ 15↓ 12↓
         24↓
     14↓  6    8         10↓  29→  7    8    5    9
  3↓
18→  1    8    7    2         10→  2    1    4    3
21→  2    7    9    3    11↓      3→   2    1        10↓
              4→   1    3         4↓ 16↓  4→   3    1
  6↓ 15↓  5↓
45→  5    6    3    4    8    1    7    2    9
12→  1    9    2         12→  3    9
```

Page 134

```
                   9↓   6↓              18↓ 16↓
            3→   1    2         17→  8    9
         41↓                11↓                 42↓
     42→  4    8    3    9    6    7    5
  17↓
16→  9    7    7→   1    2    4    13→  4    9
              6↓                    6↓
13→  8    2    3              19→  2    9    8
         6→   5    1         11→  3    8
  16↓                                            3↓
19→  9    8    2    21↓ 16↓ 11↓ 10→  1    7    2
16→  7    9    24→  7    9    8    7→   6    1
              9↓                    5↓
     28→  6    2    5    7    1    4    3
            16→  7    9    3→   2    1
```

Page 135

```
     4↓  17↓ 32↓ 22↓                   27↓  4↓
27→  3    9    8    7              4→   1    3
                              11↓
20→  1    8    5    6         7→   4    2    1
            16→  7    9    24→  9    7    8
         22↓            11↓                      16↓
     16→  7    9    14→  8    6    12→  3    9
  4↓              23↓            35↓
45→  1    5    3    9    2    8    6    4    7
5→   3    2    7→   6    1    17→  8    9
              16↓            21↓
         20→  3    9    8    16→  7    9
  3↓                                   16↓  17↓
12→  1    4    7         29→  8    5    7    9
3→   2    1              30→  6    7    9    8
```

Page 136

```
                   16↓  24↓              15↓  40↓
            16→   9    7         17→  8    9
  6↓ 37↓                                         18↓
29→  5    9    7    8         19→  4    6    9
                         4↓   3↓
6→   1    5    27→  9    1    2    3    4    8
            4↓
     5→   2    3    4→   3    1    3→   2    1
                                   10↓
  4↓      3    1         16→  9    7
  6↓              16↓ 11↓
4→   3    1    17→  9    8    4→   1    3
            23↓              8↓                  12↓
23→  1    4    6    7    3    2    17→  8    9
                                   5↓
18→  2    7    9         11→  5    2    1    3
     14→  6    8         4→   1    3
```

Page 137

17↓ 4↓ 34↓   17↓ 3↓ 22↓

15→ 8 3 4   7→ 2 1 4   24↓
18→ 9 1 8   24→ 9 2 5 8
14↓ 15↓
30→ 9 8 7 6   8→ 1 7
35↓
30→ 9 7 6 8   16→ 7 9
15↓
13→ 7 6   8→ 5 3
14↓   3↓ 9↓
15→ 9 6   10→ 1 4 3 2
6↓
4→ 1 3   11→ 3 2 5 1
4↓   4↓ 3↓
15→ 4 8 1 2   6→ 2 3 1
6→ 2 3 1   7→ 4 1 2

Page 138

4↓ 24↓ 45↓ 5↓

18→ 1 8 6 3   4↓
22→ 3 9 7 2 1   24↓
20↓ 34↓
17→ 9 8   10→ 7 3   10→ 3 7   29↓
3↓
9→ 2 6 1   5→ 2 3   6→ 1 5
16↓   11↓
45→ 6 7 2 9 4 1 3 5 8
7→ 3 4   16→ 7 9   24→ 8 9 7
15↓   23↓
17→ 9 8   17→ 8 9   11→ 2 9
17↓   16↓
35→ 7 8 5 6 9
25→ 9 1 8 7

Page 139

10↓ 9↓ 34↓   16↓ 16↓ 30↓

22→ 9 7 6   24→ 8 7 9   23↓
7→ 1 2 4   28→ 5 9 6 8
15↓ 10↓
21→ 7 9 2 3   17→ 8 9
36↓
30→ 7 9 6 8   7→ 1 6
17→ 9 8   33↓
6↓   7→ 5 2
4→ 3 1   5↓ 4↓
8→ 2 6   16→ 3 1 8 4
10→ 1 2 3 4
4↓
11→ 1 5 3 2   23→ 9 6 8
14↓ 17↓
13→ 8 1 4   24→ 7 8 9

Page 140

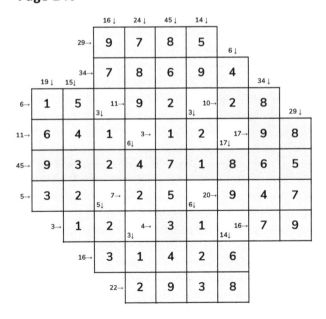

16↓ 24↓ 45↓ 14↓

29→ 9 7 8 5   6↓
34→ 7 8 6 9 4   34↓
19↓ 15↓
6→ 1 5   11→ 9 2   10→ 2 8   29↓
3↓   3↓
11→ 6 4 1   3→ 1 2   17→ 9 8
6↓   17↓
45→ 9 3 2 4 7 1 8 6 5
5→ 3 2   7→ 2 5   20→ 9 4 7
5↓   6↓
3→ 1 2   4→ 3 1   16→ 7 9
3↓   14↓
16→ 3 1 4 2 6
22→ 2 9 3 8

Page 141

Top clues: 15↓ 17↓ 28↓ 7↓ 4↓ 22↓

- 23→ 8 9 6 | 6→ 1 3 2 | 14↓
- 24→ 7 8 9 | 10→ 4 1 3 2
- 15↓ 17↓ — 24→ 5 9 8 2 | 4→ 1 3
- 23↓ 30→ 8 7 6 9 | 16→ 7 9
- 16↓ 4→ 3 1 | 8→ 3 5
- 6↓ 5→ 1 4 | 4↓ 17↓
- 3→ 2 1 | 17→ 3 8 2 4
- 7↓ 18→ 2 1 9 6 | 3↓ 17↓
- 11→ 3 5 2 1 | 14→ 4 1 9
- 7→ 2 1 4 | 11→ 1 2 8

Page 142

Top clues: 4↓ 18↓ 22↓ 43↓

- 4→ 3 1 | 17→ 8 9 | 23↓
- 7↓ 36↓ 22→ 6 7 1 8 | 18→ 9 3 6
- 8↓ 5↓ 3→ 1 2 | 39→ 9 6 4 5 7 8
- 17↓ 14→ 6 8 | 3→ 2 1 | 15→ 6 9
- 16↓ 13→ 4 9 | 15→ 7 8
- 23↓ 4↓ 3↓ 11→ 6 5 | 4→ 3 1 | 13→ 9 4
- 15↓ 15↓ 12↓ 23→ 8 3 5 1 2 4 | 14→ 5 9
- 3↓ 24→ 9 8 7 | 11→ 5 2 1 3
- 4→ 1 3 | 7→ 6 1

Page 143

Top clues: 16↓ 7↓ 45↓ 3↓

- 17→ 9 2 5 1
- 17↓ 24→ 7 4 3 2 8
- 10↓ 20↓ 35↓ 4→ 1 3 | 10→ 1 9 | 15→ 9 6
- 17↓ 16↓ 22↓ 15→ 4 2 9 | 15→ 8 7 | 17→ 8 9
- 7↓ 3↓ 45→ 3 6 8 4 2 9 1 7 5
- 3→ 2 1 | 4→ 3 1 | 8→ 2 5 1
- 17↓ 24↓ 17→ 8 9 | 16→ 7 9 | 16→ 9 7
- 16↓ 15↓ 34→ 8 9 4 7 6
- 30→ 7 6 8 9

Page 144

Top clues: 8↓ 3↓ 21↓ 4↓

- 4→ 3 1 | 7→ 4 3
- 3↓ 42↓ 28↓ 11→ 1 3 5 2 | 6→ 3 1 2
- 17↓ 3↓ 11→ 2 9 | 11→ 9 2 | 5→ 3 2
- 4↓ 22↓ 23→ 7 3 4 8 1 | 7→ 6 1
- 17↓ 14→ 6 1 7 | 21→ 5 9 7
- 3↓ 10↓ 5→ 1 4 | 32→ 5 9 6 8 4 | 3↓
- 10→ 2 8 | 3→ 2 1 | 6→ 5 1
- 6↓ 4↓ 8↓ 12→ 5 4 3 | 11→ 3 5 1 2
- 3→ 2 1 | 4→ 1 3

Page 145

Kakuro solution grid (clues → answers):

- 23→ 6 9 8 17→ 9 8
- 38→ 2 8 5 6 1 4 3 9
- 4→ 3 1   7→ 5 2
- 6→ 4 2   17→ 1 9 7
- 8→ 1 4 3   23→ 8 6 9
- 13→ 7 1 5   16→ 9 7
- 3→ 1 2   4→ 1 3
- 44→ 3 9 6 7 8 4 5 2
- 17→ 9 8   24→ 8 9 7

Down clues: 11↓ 15↓ 14↓ 12↓ 17↓ 10↓ 22↓ 7↓ 17↓ 28↓ 4↓ 21↓ 12↓ 17↓ 3↓ 12↓ 17↓ 4↓ 17↓ 11↓

Page 146

Kakuro solution grid (clues → answers):

- 23→ 6 8 9   17→ 8 9
- 44→ 5 2 9 6 7 3 4 8
- 5→ 1 4   4→ 3 1
- 8→ 2 6   23→ 8 6 9
- 6→ 3 1 2   23→ 8 6 9
- 6→ 3 1 2   15→ 7 8
- 17→ 8 9   14→ 8 6
- 36→ 2 4 3 8 1 6 5 7
- 17→ 9 8   10→ 6 3 1

Down clues: 15↓ 14↓ 19↓ 12↓ 17↓ 11↓ 16↓ 12↓ 14↓ 35↓ 3↓ 30↓ 13↓ 11↓ 12↓ 4↓ 7↓

Page 147

Kakuro solution grid (clues → answers):

- 14→ 2 1 3 8   10→ 1 9
- 15→ 1 3 5 6   20→ 7 5 8
- 17→ 8 9   16→ 1 9 6
- 8→ 6 2   5→ 3 2   3→ 2 1
- 45→ 6 8 9 7 1 4 5 3 2
- 12→ 9 3   11→ 9 2   5→ 1 4
- 18→ 9 1 8   3→ 1 2
- 8→ 1 5 2   23→ 3 4 7 9
- 16→ 9 7   22→ 2 3 9 8

Down clues: 3↓ 4↓ 27↓ 23↓ 21↓ 17↓ 16↓ 7↓ 17↓ 38↓ 6↓ 3↓ 8↓ 15↓ 24↓ 15↓ 3↓ 6↓ 16↓ 17↓ 10↓

Page 150: Love Thy Neighbor

In this encoding, each letter is swapped with its "neighbor" in the alphabet: A and B are swapped, C and D are swapped, and so on.
The answer:

Remember, if you ever need a helping hand, you'll find one at the end of your arm. As you grow older, you will discover that you have two hands: one for helping yourself, the other for helping others.

—*Antoine de Saint–Exupéry*, The Little Prince

Page 150: Second Shift

The clue to this puzzle is in the title, "Second Shift." In this encryption, each letter is shifted forward 2 letters of the alphabet: A becomes C, B becomes D, and so on. This type of cipher is known as a Caesar cipher.
The original message is:

There is no time for cut-and-dried monotony. There is time for work. And time for love. That leaves no other time.

—*Coco Chanel*

Page 151: Puzzle Number Three

Start with a Caesar shift of three, given the title of the puzzle. This gives you the following message:

Apply another Caesar shift of 12:

MZP MZAFTQD EQHQZ, MRFQD DQYAHUZS SE MZP JE. PASXG T IHJXM WSBZL ABSFLXEJY BJGMH T ASHEX, AX WHJXLGSM VSEBFU HJNM. AJX WBZSL WJXXISXK, XGSCJHRL MASX LVJXGXKR, TSGW VJHFXL HSNM MAJX HMSAXK LBJWX XGJEBSZAMXGJXJW.

And another seven, after removing Gs and Xs.

DOGLU H WVXLA KGPNZ OPGTZLSXM PXUAV H OGVSL, OL KVXLZUGA JGSPIL VXBA. OXL KPNGZ KXLLWGLY, LUGQXVFZ AOGL ZJXLULYF, HGUK JXVTLZ VGBA AOXL VAGOLY ZPXKL LUXSPGNOALUXLXK.

Following these instructions, remove all Gs and Xs from the remaining ciphertext:

DOLU H WVLA KPNZ OPTZLSM PUAV H OVSL, OL KVLZUA JSPTI VBA. OL KPNZ KLLWLY, LUQVFZ AOL ZJLULYF, HUK JVTLZ VBA AOL VAOLY ZPKL LUSPNOALULK.

And shift each letter of the alphabet by 7 to decode the final answer:

When a poet digs himself into a hole, he doesn't climb out. He digs deeper, enjoys the scenery, and comes out the other side enlightened.

—*Criss Jami*, Venus in Arms

Page 151: That's Odd

To decode this message, only read the odd-numbered letters in the speech (first = T, third = H, etc.)

The snow goose need not bathe to make itself white. Neither need you do anything but be yourself.

—*Lao Tzu*

Page 152: Element of Surprise

The key to this puzzle is in the periodic table. Each letter of the original message has been replaced with the chemical symbol for a corresponding element: So A becomes H, B becomes He, C becomes Li, and so on. Reversing that process decodes the original message:

No amount of experimentation can ever prove me right; a single experiment can prove me wrong.

—*Albert Einstein*

Page 152: Unscramble

Unscramble each of the given chunks to get the following:

You must live in the present, launch yourself on every wave, find your eternity in each moment. Fools stand on their island of opportunities and look toward another land. There is no other land; there is no other life but this.

—*Henry Thoreau*

Page 153: Unscramble, Grown-Up

Unscramble each of the given chunks to get the following:

If you were to say to the grown-ups, "I saw a beautiful house made of rosy brick, with geraniums in the windows and doves on the roof," they would not be able to get any idea of that house at all. You would have to say to them, "I saw a house that cost $20,000." Then they would exclaim, "Oh, what a pretty house that is!" They are like that. One must not hold it against them. Children should always show great forbearance toward grown-up people.

—*Antoine de Saint–Exupéry*, The Little Prince

Page 153: TV Channels

Each letter of the alphabet is replaced with a corresponding prime number: A=2, B=3, C=5, D=7, and so on. The decoded plaintext is:

Hollywood's a place where they'll pay you a thousand dollars for a kiss, and fifty cents for your soul.

—*Marilyn Monroe*

Page 154: War of the Words

Each letter of the alphabet is replaced with a set of letters from its NATO phonetic alphabet counterpart. For example, A ("Alfa") is "Lfa," and B ("Bravo") is "Rav." The final solution is:

Ultimate excellence lies not in winning every battle, but in defeating the enemy without ever fighting.

—*Sun Tzu*, The Art of War

Page 154: Arrows

The first step is to format the ciphertext with 40 characters (8 groups of 5) per row. You can then crack this transposition cipher by starting from the bottom left corner of the ciphertext and reading the letters in an up-and-down snaking pattern, alternating directions with each column. The decoded text is:

One thing I've learned through all the ups and downs is that if you're doing things right, then you have a core group of people. Not just a core group like your homies or your buddies, but a group of people that has a good influence on you, who you respect and admire, and you know that if they're on your side, you're doing something right.

—*Hope Solo*

Page 155: This Week's Stock Market

For each stock's ticker, shift the letters in the ticker by the given number, e.g., "BNOC +.05." would require you to shift each of B, N, O, and C five letters forward in the alphabet to get GSTH. To fully reconstruct the answer, put the five tickers in order, starting from Monday and ending with Friday:

Too many people spend money they haven't earned to buy things they don't want to impress people they don't like.

—*Will Rogers*

Page 155: Numskull's Numscramble

Unscramble the digits into two-digit blocks, each of which corresponds to a letter of the alphabet: 01=A, 02=B, and so on. The correct ordering of the digits is:

01 031513131514 13091920011105 20080120
160515161205 13011105 23081514 201825091407
2015 040519090714 191513052008091407
03151316120520051225 061515121618151506
0919 2015 21140405180519200913012005 200805
091407051421092025 1506 0315131612052005
0615151219

Which translates to this final message:

A common mistake that people make when trying to design something completely foolproof is to underestimate the ingenuity of complete fools.

—*Douglas Adams, Mostly Harmless*

Page 156: Numskull's New Numscramble

The decryption mechanism is the same as in "Numskull's Numscramble." The final message is:

The reasonable man adapts himself to the world; the unreasonable one persists in trying to adapt the world to himself. Therefore all progress depends on the unreasonable man.

—*George Bernard Shaw*

Page 156: Notably Nastier Numscramble

I don't believe in an afterlife, so I don't have to spend my whole life fearing hell, or fearing heaven even more. For whatever the tortures of hell, I think the boredom of heaven would be even worse.

—*Isaac Asimov*

Page 157: The Joy of Music

Each different note or rest symbol represents a letter of the alphabet. The final answer is:

If you are a chef, no matter how good a chef you are, it's not good cooking for yourself; the joy is in cooking for others—it's the same with music.

—*will.i.am*

Page 157: You're On Your Own

This is a substitution cipher in which each letter of the alphabet is replaced with a different one. The decoded message is:

I need to see my own beauty and to continue to be reminded that I am enough, that I am worthy of love without effort, that I am beautiful, that the texture of my hair and that the shape of my curves, the size of my lips, the color of my skin, and the feelings that I have are all worthy and okay.

—*Tracee Ellis Ross*

Page 158: You're Still On Your Own

Like the previous puzzle, this cryptogram is also a substitution cipher. The decoded message is:

Whatever course you decide upon, there is always someone to tell you that you are wrong. There are always difficulties arising which tempt you to believe that your critics are right. To map out a course of action and follow it to an end requires courage.

—*Ralph Waldo Emerson*

Page 158: Tough Times

Another substitution cipher, similar to the previous two:

My dad was our rock. Although he was diagnosed with multiple sclerosis in his early 30s, he was our provider, our champion, our hero. As he got sicker, it got harder for him to walk, it took him longer to get dressed in the morning. But if he was in pain, he never let on. He never stopped smiling and laughing—even while struggling to button his shirt, even while using two canes to get himself across the room to give my mom a kiss. He just woke up a little earlier and worked a little harder.

—Michelle Obama

Page 159: Don't Wait for A Sign

This puzzle may look funny with all the symbols, but it's just another substitution cipher:

Our uniqueness makes us special, makes perception valuable—but it can also make us lonely. This loneliness is different from being 'alone': You can be lonely even surrounded by people. The feeling I'm talking about stems from the sense that we can never fully share the truth of who we are. I experienced this acutely at an early age.

—Amy Tan

Page 159: Nobody Will Help You

This puzzle is also a substitution cipher, but with the letters reversed as an added layer of obfuscation.

Would you like me to give you a formula for success? It's quite simple, really: Double your rate of failure. You are thinking of failure as the enemy of success. But it isn't at all. You can be discouraged by failure or you can learn from it, so go ahead and make mistakes. Make all you can. Because remember that's where you will find success.

—Thomas J. Watson

Page 160: No Two Ways About It

Each letter in the cipher text represents a numerical digit; pairs of digits then represent plaintext letters. For example, U (ciphertext) represents 2, so UU would decode to the 22nd letter of the alphabet (V). The decoded text is:

Vision without action is merely a dream. Action without vision just passes the time. Vision with action can change the world.

—Joel A. Barker

Page 160: The Mother of All Cryptograms

First, solve the substitution cipher to obtain:

In the following text, every fifth word will be reversed, starting with "baby":

When you hold your ybab in your arms the tsrif time, and you think fo all the things you nac say and do to ecneulfni him, it's a tremendous ytilibisnopser. What you do with mih can influence not only mih, but everyone he meets dna not for a day ro a month or a raey but for time and ytinrete.

After reversing every fifth word, the final plaintext is as follows:

When you hold your baby in your arms the first time, and you think of all the things you can say and do to influence him, it's a tremendous responsibility. What you do with him can influence not only him, but everyone he meets and not for a day or a month or a year but for time and eternity.

—Rose Kennedy

FURTHER PUZZLING

If you enjoyed the variety format of this book, you might also enjoy *Puzzler*, a UK magazine that features crosswords, word searches, sudokus, and more. Even if you don't subscribe to the print magazine, you can find a plethora of online puzzles on their website and app.

Many mainstream publications also feature puzzle sections; for example, the *New York Times* is most famous for its high-quality crossword puzzles, but also publishes sudoku and Calcudoku puzzles online.

If you particularly gravitated toward one category of puzzle, you can search online for specialized resources for that category. There are a number of sites that generate puzzles of various grid sizes and difficulty levels and provide an interface to solve the puzzles directly on the website—for example, Newdoku.com (for Calcudoku), KakuroConquest.com (for Kakuro), and RazzlePuzzles.com (for word search, Calcudoku, cryptograms, and sudoku).

Of course, there are many more categories of puzzles beyond the ones in this book. In fact, there's a genre of freeform puzzles in which there are no clear instructions for each puzzle—figuring out the instructions is part of the challenge! To get started with these, I recommend checking out the Puzzled Pint, a casual in-person event hosted monthly at pubs and bars across many cities (see PuzzledPint.com). I also run a website, MissionStreetPuzzles.com, with some examples of these.

Happy puzzling!

ACKNOWLEDGMENTS

Thank you, reader, for taking the time to peruse this book.

Thank you to the Mission Street Puzzles community for your amazing loyalty, creativity, and puzzle-solving prowess.

Thank you to every puzzle author who has stumped me with your ingenuity.

And finally, acknowledgements for the four most important people in my life:

Thank you to Sean for contributing some of the puzzles in this book, for thoughtful feedback along the way, and for supporting me at every step.

Thank you to Bryant, for always having the right words.

Thank you to Daddy, for always having the right logic.

Thank you to Mommy, for always being right.

And infinite thanks to all four of you, for your love, encouragement, and confidence in me. You made this book possible—I hope you enjoyed it!

ABOUT THE AUTHOR

Willa Chen is a software engineer at Google who creates and solves puzzles in her spare time. She is the founder of Mission Street Puzzles, an online puzzle competition that highlights local gems in cities around the world. Willa grew up in Michigan and now lives in the San Francisco Bay Area. Other than doing puzzles, Willa also enjoys playing board games, climbing rocks, and spending time with family.